ONE-ACT PLAYS
OF TO-DAY ✦ ✦
✦ ✦ ✦   FIRST SERIES

ONE-ACT PLAYS OF TO-DAY

FIRST SERIES
Selected by J. W. MARRIOTT

One Act Plays in Reprint

Core Collection Books, inc.
GREAT NECK, NEW YORK

First Published 1924
Reprinted 1978

International Standard Book Number 0-8486-2039-9

Library of Congress — Catalog Card No. 77-094346

PRINTED IN THE UNITED STATES OF AMERICA

FOREWORD

THIS little volume of one-act plays—the first of its kind to be published in England—consists of eleven short plays by eminent modern English, Scottish, and Irish playwrights. With one exception they are written in prose; they contain no words that have become obsolete or have changed their meaning; there are no obscure allusions that belong to a different century; their language is as familiar as that of the newspapers and magazines; and their outlook is essentially that of the present day.

The one-act play which can be read aloud in twenty minutes or half an hour shows how a single theme can be presented, developed, and brought to a climax with the minimum of material and the maximum of dramatic effect. Classical five-act plays usually contain three or more interweaving stories, and the continual change of scene and 'jumping' from plot to plot tend to bewilder. The one-act play is ideal as a first step in the appreciation of drama.

It is fortunate that the one-act play is now accepted as a legitimate form of dramatic art—as legitimate as the short story or the miniature—and that the playwrights who are still working in our midst have already produced such a quantity of excellent short plays.

The plays in this book are greatly varied; they range from light comedy to fantasy, from farce to tragedy. They may be read, analysed, discussed, and studied in private; but they may not be acted in public without first securing permission and paying the necessary fees.   J. W. M.

ACKNOWLEDGMENTS

THE compiler desires to express his thanks to the following authors and publishers for the permission given to print the plays in this volume:
Mr A. A. Milne and Messrs Chatto and Windus for "The Boy Comes Home," from *First Plays*; Mr Harold Brighouse and Messrs Gowans and Gray, Ltd., for "Followers"; Mr Arnold Bennett for "The Stepmother," from *Polite Farces*; the heir of the late Captain Oliphant Down and Messrs Gowans and Gray, Ltd., for "The Maker of Dreams"; Mr John Galsworthy and Messrs Duckworth and Co. for "The Little Man," from *Six Short Plays*; Lord Dunsany and Messrs Elkin Mathews, Ltd., for "A Night at an Inn," from *Plays of Gods and Men*; Mr J. A. Ferguson and Messrs Gowans and Gray, Ltd., for "Campbell of Kilmhor"; Mr Allan Monkhouse for "The Grand Cham's Diamond"; Mr J. J. Bell and Messrs Gowans and Gray, Ltd., for "Thread o' Scarlet"; Miss Olive Conway for "Becky Sharp"; Mr John Drinkwater and Messrs Sidgwick and Jackson, Ltd., for "$X=0$: A Night of the Trojan War," from *Pawns*.

Note.—The plays in this volume are fully protected by copyright. Addresses to which applications for permission to perform should be sent will be found at the end of each play.

CONTENTS

		PAGE
THE BOY COMES HOME	*A. A. Milne*	11
FOLLOWERS	*Harold Brighouse*	37
THE STEPMOTHER	*Arnold Bennett*	57
THE MAKER OF DREAMS	*Oliphant Down*	83
THE LITTLE MAN	*John Galsworthy*	107
A NIGHT AT AN INN	*Lord Dunsany*	135
CAMPBELL OF KILMHOR	*J. A. Ferguson*	153
THE GRAND CHAM'S DIAMOND	*Allan Monkhouse*	173
THREAD O' SCARLET	*J. J. Bell*	199
BECKY SHARP	*Olive Conway*	219
X = 0: A NIGHT OF THE TROJAN WAR	*John Drinkwater*	241

THE BOY COMES HOME

A COMEDY IN ONE ACT

BY A. A. MILNE

Mr A. A. MILNE became a journalist on leaving Cambridge, and was the assistant-editor of *Punch* at the age of twenty-four. On the outbreak of war in 1914 he entered the Army, and it was during his leisure hours as a professional soldier that he first began to write plays. Other subalterns spent their spare time in golf and bridge: Mr Milne's new game was far more exciting.

He began with one-act plays, including "The Boy Comes Home," but his reputation as a dramatist rests upon "Mr Pim Passes By" and "The Truth about Blayds" (especially Act I). His characters are the pleasant people one may meet in an English country house. He excels in dialogue.

It seems natural that a regular contributor to *Punch* should write in a vein of light comedy, and Mr Milne has a delightfully easy touch and a charm which cannot be defined.

The following play was written when the author was thirty-four.

CHARACTERS

UNCLE JAMES
AUNT EMILY
PHILIP
MARY
MRS HIGGINS

This play was first produced by Mr Owen Nares at the Victoria Palace Theatre, London, on September 9, 1918, with the following cast:

Philip	OWEN NARES
Uncle James	TOM REYNOLDS
Aunt Emily	DOROTHY RADFORD
Mary	ADAH DICK
Mrs Higgins	RACHEL DE SOLLA

THE BOY COMES HOME

Scene: *A room in* Uncle James's *house in the Cromwell Road.*

Time: *The day after the War.*

Any room in Uncle James's *house is furnished in heavy mid-Victorian style; this particular morning-room is perhaps solider and more respectable even than the others, from the heavy table in the middle of it to the heavy engravings on the walls. There are two doors to it. The one at the back opens into the hall, the one at the side into the dining-room.*

Philip *comes in from the hall and goes into the dining-room. Apparently he finds nothing there, for he returns to the morning-room, looks about him for a moment and then rings the bell. It is ten o'clock, and he wants his breakfast. He picks up the paper, and sits in a heavy armchair in front of the fire—a pleasant-looking well-built person of twenty-three, with an air of decisiveness about him.* Mary, *the parlour-maid, comes in.*

Mary. Did you ring, Master Philip?

Philip [*absently*]. Yes; I want some breakfast, please, Mary.

Mary [*coldly*]. Breakfast has been cleared away an hour ago.

Philip. Exactly. That's why I rang. You can boil me a couple of eggs or something. And coffee, not tea.

MARY. I'm sure I don't know what Mrs Higgins will say?

PHILIP [*getting up*]. Who is Mrs Higgins?

MARY. The cook. And she's not used to being put about like this.

PHILIP. Do you think she'll say something?

MARY. I don't know *what* she'll say.

PHILIP. You needn't tell me, you know, if you don't want to. Anyway, I don't suppose it will shock me. One gets used to it in the Army. [*He smiles pleasantly at her.*]

MARY. Well, I'll do what I can, sir. But breakfast at eight sharp is the master's rule, just as it used to be before you went away to the war.

PHILIP. Before I went away to the war I did a lot of silly things. Don't drag them up now. [*More curtly*] Two eggs, and if there's a ham bring that along too. [*He turns away.*]

MARY [*doubtfully, as she prepares to go*]. Well, I'm sure I don't know what Mrs Higgins will say. [*Exit* MARY.

[*As she goes out she makes way for* AUNT EMILY *to come in, a kind-hearted mid-Victorian lady who has never had any desire for the vote.*

EMILY. *There* you are, Philip! Good-morning, dear. Did you sleep well?

PHILIP. Rather; splendidly, thanks, Aunt Emily. How are you? [*He kisses her.*]

EMILY. And did you have a good breakfast? Naughty boy to be late for it. I always thought they had to get up so early in the Army.

PHILIP. They do. That's why they're so late when they get out of the Army.

EMILY. Dear me! I should have thought a habit of four years would have stayed with you.

PHILIP. Every morning for four years, as I've shot out of bed, I've said to myself, "Wait! A time will come." [*Smiling*] That doesn't really give a habit a chance.

EMILY. Well, I daresay you wanted your sleep out. I was so afraid that a really cosy bed would keep you awake after all those years in the trenches.

PHILIP. Well, one isn't in the trenches all the time. And one gets leave—if one's an officer.

EMILY [*reproachfully*]. You didn't spend much of it with *us*, Philip.

PHILIP [*taking her hands*]. I know; but you did understand, didn't you, dear?

EMILY. We're not very gay, and I know you must have wanted gaiety for the little time you had. But I think your Uncle James felt it. After all, dear, you've lived with us for some years, and he *is* your guardian.

PHILIP. I know. *You've* been a darling to me always, Aunt Emily. But [*awkwardly*] Uncle James and I——

EMILY. Of course, he is a *little* difficult to get on with. I'm more used to him. But I'm sure he really is very fond of you, Philip.

PHILIP. H'm! I always used to be frightened of him. . . . I suppose he's just the same. He seemed just the same last night—and he still has breakfast at eight o'clock. Been making pots of money, I suppose?

EMILY. He never tells me exactly, but he did speak once about the absurdity of the excess-profits tax. You see, jam is a thing the Army wants.

PHILIP. It certainly gets it.

EMILY. It was so nice for him, because it made him feel he was doing his bit, helping the poor men in the trenches.

Enter MARY

MARY. Mrs Higgins wishes to speak to you, ma'am. [*She looks at* PHILIP *as much as to say,* " *There you are!* "]

EMILY [*getting up*]. Yes, I'll come. [*To* PHILIP] I think I'd better just see what she wants, Philip.

PHILIP [*firmly to* MARY]. Tell Mrs Higgins to come here. [MARY *hesitates and looks at her mistress.*] At once, please. [*Exit* MARY.

EMILY [*upset*]. Philip, dear, I don't know what Mrs Higgins will say——

PHILIP. No; nobody seems to. I thought we might really find out for once.

EMILY [*going towards the door*]. Perhaps I'd better go——

PHILIP [*putting his arm round her waist*]. Oh no, you mustn't. You see, she really wants to see *me*.

EMILY. *You?*

PHILIP. Yes; I ordered breakfast five minutes ago.

EMILY. Philip! My poor boy! Why didn't you tell me? and I daresay I could have got it for you. Though I don't know what Mrs Higgins——

[*An extremely angry voice is heard outside, and* MRS HIGGINS, *stout and aggressive, comes in.*

MRS HIGGINS [*truculently*]. You sent for me, ma'am?

EMILY [*nervously*]. Yes—er—I think if you—perhaps——

PHILIP [*calmly*]. *I* sent for you, Mrs Higgins. I want some breakfast. Didn't Mary tell you?

MRS HIGGINS. Breakfast is at eight o'clock. It always has been as long as I've been in this house, and always will be until I get further orders.

PHILIP. Well, you've just got further orders. Two eggs, and if there's a ham——

MRS HIGGINS. Orders. We're talking about orders. From whom in this house do I take orders, may I ask?

THE BOY COMES HOME

PHILIP. In this case from me.

MRS HIGGINS [*playing her trump-card*]. In that case, ma'am, I wish to give a month's notice from to-day. *In*clusive.

PHILIP [*quickly, before his aunt can say anything*]. Certainly. In fact, you'd probably prefer it if my aunt gave *you* notice, and then you could go at once. We can easily arrange that. [*To* AUNT EMILY *as he takes out a fountain-pen and cheque-book*] What do you pay her?

EMILY [*faintly*]. Forty-five pounds.

PHILIP [*writing on his knee*]. Twelves into forty-five . . . [*Pleasantly to* MRS HIGGINS, *but without looking up*]! hope you don't mind a Cox's cheque. Some people do; but this is quite a good one. [*Tearing it out*] Here you are.

MRS HIGGINS [*taken aback*]. What's this?

PHILIP. Your wages instead of notice. Now you can go at once.

MRS HIGGINS. Who said anything about going?

PHILIP [*surprised*]. I'm sorry; I thought *you* did.

MRS HIGGINS. If it's only a bit of breakfast, I don't say but what I mightn't get it, if I'm asked decent.

PHILIP [*putting back the cheque*]. Then let me say again, "Two eggs, ham and coffee." And Mary can bring the ham up at once, and I'll get going on that. [*Turning away*] Thanks very much.

MRS HIGGINS. Well, I—well—well! [*Exit speechless.*

PHILIP [*surprised*]. Is that all she ever says? It isn't much to worry about.

EMILY. Philip, how could you! I should have been terrified.

PHILIP. Well, you see, I've done your job for two years out there.

EMILY. What job?

PHILIP. Mess President. . . . I think I'll go and see about that ham.

> [*He smiles at her and goes out into the dining-room.* AUNT EMILY *wanders round the room, putting a few things tidy as is her habit, when she is interrupted by the entrance of* UNCLE JAMES. JAMES *is not a big man, nor an impressive one in his black morning-coat; and his thin straggly beard, now going grey, does not hide a chin of any great power; but he has a severity which passes for strength with the weak.*]

JAMES. Philip down yet?

EMILY. He's just having his breakfast.

JAMES [*looking at his watch*]. Ten o'clock. [*Snapping it shut and putting it back*] Ten o'clock. I say ten o'clock, Emily.

EMILY. Yes, dear, I heard you.

JAMES. You don't say anything?

EMILY [*vaguely*]. I expect he's tired after that long war.

JAMES. That's no excuse for not being punctual. I suppose he learnt punctuality in the Army?

EMILY. I expect he learnt it, James, but I understood him to say that he'd forgotten it.

JAMES. Then the sooner he learns it again the better. I particularly stayed away from the office to-day in order to talk things over with him, and [*looking at his watch*] here's ten o'clock—past ten—and no sign of him. I'm practically throwing away a day.

EMILY. What are you going to talk to him about?

JAMES. His future, naturally. I have decided that the best thing he can do is to come into the business at once.

EMILY. Are you really going to talk it over with him, James, or are you just going to tell him that he *must* come?

THE BOY COMES HOME

JAMES [*surprised*]. What do you mean? What's the difference? Naturally we shall talk it over first, and—er—naturally he'll fall in with my wishes.

EMILY. I suppose he can hardly help himself, poor boy.

JAMES. Not until he's twenty-five, anyhow. When he's twenty-five he can have his own money and do what he likes with it.

EMILY [*timidly*]. But I think you ought to consult him a little, dear. After all, he *has* been fighting for us.

JAMES [*with his back to the fire*]. Now that's the sort of silly sentiment that there's been much too much of. I object to it strongly. I don't want to boast, but I think I may claim to have done my share. I gave up my nephew to my country, and I—er—suffered from the shortage of potatoes to an extent that you probably didn't realize. Indeed, if it hadn't been for your fortunate discovery about that time that you didn't really like potatoes, I don't know how we should have carried on. And, as I think I've told you before, the excess-profits tax seemed to me a singularly stupid piece of legislation—but I paid it. And I don't go boasting about how much I paid.

EMILY [*unconvinced*]. Well, I think that Philip's four years out there have made him more of a man; he doesn't seem somehow like a boy who can be told what to do. I'm sure they've taught him something.

JAMES. I've no doubt that they've taught him something about—er—bombs and—er—which end a revolver goes off, and how to form fours. But I don't see that that sort of thing helps him to decide upon the most suitable career for a young man in after-war conditions.

EMILY. Well, I can only say you'll find him different.

JAMES. I didn't notice any particular difference last night.

EMILY. I think you'll find him rather more—I can't

quite think of the word, but Mrs Higgins could tell you what I mean.

JAMES. Of course, if he likes to earn his living any other way, he may; but I don't see how he proposes to do it so long as I hold the purse-strings. [*Looking at his watch*] Perhaps you'd better tell him that I cannot wait any longer.

[EMILY *opens the door leading into the dining-room and talks through it to* PHILIP.

EMILY. Philip, your uncle is waiting to see you before he goes to the office. Will you be long, dear?

PHILIP [*from the dining-room*]. Is he in a hurry?

JAMES [*shortly*]. Yes.

EMILY. He says he *is* rather, dear.

PHILIP. Couldn't he come and talk in here? It wouldn't interfere with my breakfast.

JAMES. No.

EMILY. He says he'd rather you came to *him*, darling.

PHILIP [*resigned*]. Oh, well.

EMILY [*to* JAMES]. He'll be here directly, dear. Just sit down in front of the fire and make yourself comfortable with the paper. He won't keep you long. [*She arranges him.*]

JAMES [*taking the paper*]. The morning is not the time to make oneself comfortable. It's a most dangerous habit. I nearly found myself dropping off in front of the fire just now. I don't like this hanging about, wasting the day. [*He opens the paper.*]

EMILY. You should have had a nice sleep, dear, while you could. We were up so late last night listening to Philip's stories.

JAMES. Yes, yes. [*He begins a yawn and stifles it hurriedly.*] You mustn't neglect your duties, Emily. I've no doubt you have plenty to do.

THE BOY COMES HOME

EMILY. All right, James, then I'll leave you. But don't be hard on the boy.

JAMES [*sleepily*]. I shall be just, Emily; you can rely upon that.

EMILY [*going to the door*]. I don't think that's quite what I meant. [*She goes out.*

> [JAMES, *who is now quite comfortable, begins to nod. He wakes up with a start, turns over the paper, and nods again. Soon he is breathing deeply with closed eyes.*

* * * * * *

PHILIP [*coming in*]. Sorry to have kept you waiting, but I was a bit late for breakfast. [*He takes out his pipe.*] Are we going to talk business or what?

JAMES [*taking out his watch*]. A *bit* late! I make it just two hours.

PHILIP [*pleasantly*]. All right, Uncle James. Call it two hours late. Or twenty-two hours early for to-morrow's breakfast, if you like. [*He sits down in a chair on the opposite side of the table from his uncle, and lights his pipe.*]

JAMES. You smoke now?

PHILIP [*staggered*]. I what?

JAMES [*nodding at his pipe*]. You smoke?

PHILIP. Good heavens! what do you think we *did* in France?

JAMES. Before you start smoking all over the house, I should have thought you would have asked your aunt's permission.

> [PHILIP *looks at him in amazement, and then goes to the door.*

PHILIP [*calling*]. Aunt Emily! . . . Aunt Emily! . . . Do you mind my smoking in here?

AUNT EMILY [*from upstairs*]. Of course not, darling.

PHILIP [*to* JAMES, *as he returns to his chair*]. Of course not, darling. [*He puts back his pipe in his mouth.*]

JAMES. Now, understand once and for all, Philip, while you remain in my house I expect not only punctuality, but also civility and respect. I will *not* have impertinence.

PHILIP [*unimpressed*]. Well, that's what I want to talk to you about, Uncle James. About staying in your house, I mean.

JAMES. I don't know what you do mean.

PHILIP. Well, we don't get on too well together, and I thought perhaps I'd better take rooms somewhere. You could give me an allowance until I came into my money. Or I suppose you could give me the money now if you really liked. I don't quite know how father left it to me.

JAMES [*coldly*]. You come into your money when you are twenty-five. Your father very wisely felt that to trust a large sum to a mere boy of twenty-one was simply putting temptation in his way. Whether I have the power or not to alter his dispositions, I certainly don't propose to do so.

PHILIP. If it comes to that, I *am* twenty-five.

JAMES. Indeed ? I had an impression that that event took place in about two years' time. When did you become twenty-five, may I ask ?

PHILIP [*quietly*]. It was on the Somme. We were attacking the next day and my company was in support. We were in a so-called trench on the edge of a wood—a damned rotten place to be, and we got hell. The company commander sent back to ask if we could move. The C.O. said, "Certainly not; hang on." We hung on; doing nothing, you know—just hanging on and waiting for the next day. Of course, the Boche knew all about that. He had it on us nicely. . . . [*Sadly*] Poor old Billy ! he was one of the best—our company commander, you know. They got him, poor devil ! That left *me* in command of the company. I sent a runner back to ask if I could move. Well, I'd had a bit of a scout on my own and found a sort of trench five hundred yards to the right. Not what *you'd* call a trench, of course, but compared to that wood—well, it was absolutely Hyde Park. I described the position and asked if I could go there. My man never came back. I waited an hour and sent another man. He went west too. Well, I wasn't going to send a third. It was murder. So I had to decide. We'd lost about half the company by this time, you see. Well, there were three things I could do—hang on, move to this other trench, against orders, or go back myself and explain the situation. . . . I moved. . . . And then I went back to the C.O. and told him I'd moved. . . . And then I went back to the company again. . . . [*Quietly*] That was when I became twenty-five . . . or thirty-five . . . or forty-five.

JAMES [*recovering himself with an effort*]. Ah yes, yes. [*He coughs awkwardly.*] No doubt points like that frequently crop up in the trenches. I am glad that you did well out there, and I'm sure your Colonel would speak kindly of you; but when it comes to choosing a career for you now that you have left the Army, my advice is not altogether to be despised. Your father evidently thought so, or he would not have entrusted you to my care.

PHILIP. My father didn't foresee this war.

JAMES. Yes, yes, but you make too much of this war. All you young boys seem to think you've come back from France to teach us our business. You'll find that it is you who'll have to learn, not we.

PHILIP. I'm quite prepared to learn; in fact, I want to.

JAMES. Excellent. Then we can consider that settled.

PHILIP. Well, we haven't settled yet what business I'm going to learn.

JAMES. I don't think that's very difficult. I propose to take you into my business. You'll start at the bottom, of course, but it will be a splendid opening for you.

PHILIP [*thoughtfully*]. I see. So you've decided it for me? The jam business.

JAMES [*sharply*]. Is there anything to be ashamed of in that?

PHILIP. Oh no, nothing at all. Only it doesn't happen to appeal to me.

JAMES. If you knew which side your bread was buttered, it would appeal to you very considerably.

PHILIP. I'm afraid I can't see the butter for the jam.

JAMES. I don't want any silly jokes of that sort. You were glad enough to get it out there, I've no doubt.

PHILIP. Oh yes. Perhaps that's why I'm so sick of it now. . . . No, it's no good, Uncle James; you must think of something else.

JAMES [**with a sneer**]. Perhaps *you've* thought of something else?

PHILIP. Well, I had some idea of being an architect——

JAMES. You propose to start learning to be an architect at twenty-three?

PHILIP [*smiling*]. Well, I couldn't start before, could I?

JAMES. Exactly. And now you'll find it's too late.

PHILIP. Is it? Aren't there going to be any more architects, or doctors, or solicitors, or barristers? Because we've all lost four years of our lives, are all the professions going to die out?

JAMES. And how old do you suppose you'll be before you're earning money as an architect?

PHILIP. The usual time, whatever that may be. If I'm four years behind, so is everybody else.

JAMES. Well, I think it's high time you began to earn a living at once.

THE BOY COMES HOME

PHILIP. Look here, Uncle James, do you really think that you can treat me like a boy who's just left school ? Do you think four years at the front have made no difference at all ?

JAMES. If there had been any difference, I should have expected it to take the form of an increased readiness to obey orders and recognize authority.

PHILIP [*regretfully*]. You are evidently determined to have a row. Perhaps I had better tell you once and for all that I refuse to go into the turnip and vegetable marrow business.

JAMES [*thumping the table angrily*]. And perhaps I'd better tell *you*, sir, once and for all, that I don't propose to allow rudeness from an impertinent young puppy.

PHILIP [*reminiscently*]. I remember annoying our Brigadier once. He was covered with red, had a very red face, about twenty medals, and a cold blue eye. He told me how angry he was for about five minutes while I stood to attention. I'm afraid you aren't nearly so impressive, Uncle James.

JAMES [*rather upset*]. Oh ! [*Recovering himself*] Fortunately I have other means of impressing you. The power of the purse goes a long way in this world. I propose to use it.

PHILIP. I see. . . . Yes . . . that's rather awkward, isn't it ?

JAMES [*pleasantly*]. I think you'll find it very awkward.

PHILIP [*thoughtfully*]. Yes.

    [*With an amused laugh* JAMES *settles down to his paper as if the interview were over.*

PHILIP [*to himself*]. I suppose I shall have to think of another argument. [*He takes out a revolver from his pocket and fondles it affectionately.*]

JAMES [*looking up suddenly as he is doing this—amazed*]. What on earth are you doing?

PHILIP. Souvenir from France. Do you know, Uncle James, that this revolver has killed about twenty Germans?

JAMES [*shortly*]. Oh! Well, don't go playing about with it here, or you'll be killing Englishmen before you know where you are.

PHILIP. Well, you never know. [*He raises it leisurely and points it at his uncle.*] It's a nice little weapon.

JAMES [*angrily*]. Put it down, sir. You ought to have grown out of monkey tricks like that in the Army. You ought to know better than to point an unloaded revolver at anybody. That's the way accidents always happen.

PHILIP. Not when you've been on a revolver course and know all about it. Besides, it *is* loaded.

JAMES [*very angry because he is frightened suddenly*]. Put it down at once, sir. [PHILIP *turns it away from him and examines it carelessly.*] What's the matter with you? Have you gone mad suddenly?

PHILIP [*mildly*]. I thought you'd be interested in it. It's shot such a lot of Germans.

JAMES. Well, it won't want to shoot any more, and the sooner you get rid of it the better.

PHILIP. I wonder. Does it ever occur to you, Uncle James, that there are about a hundred thousand people in England who own revolvers, who are quite accustomed to them and—who have nobody to practise on now?

JAMES. No, sir, it certainly doesn't.

PHILIP [*thoughtfully*]. I wonder if it will make any difference. You know, one gets so used to potting at people. It's rather difficult to realize suddenly that one oughtn't to.

JAMES [*getting up*]. I don't know what the object of all

THE BOY COMES HOME

this tomfoolery is, if it has one. But you understand that I expect you to come to the office with me to-morrow at nine o'clock. Kindly see that you're punctual. [*He turns to go away.*]

PHILIP [*softly*]. Uncle James.

JAMES [*over his shoulder*]. I have no more——

PHILIP [*in his parade voice*]. Damn it, sir! stand to attention when you talk to an officer! [JAMES *instinctively turns round and stiffens himself.*] That's better; you can sit down if you like. [*He motions* JAMES *to his chair with the revolver.*]

JAMES [*going nervously to his chair*]. What does this bluff mean?

PHILIP. It isn't bluff, it's quite serious. [*Pointing the revolver at his uncle*] Do sit down.

JAMES [*sitting down*]. Threats, eh?

PHILIP. Persuasion.

JAMES. At the point of the revolver? You settle your arguments by force? Good heavens, sir! this is just the very thing that we were fighting to put down.

PHILIP. *We* were fighting! *We! We!* Uncle, you're a humorist.

JAMES. Well, "you," if you prefer it. Although those of us who stayed at home——

PHILIP. Yes, never mind about the excess profits now. I can tell you quite well what we fought for. We used force to put down force. That's what I'm doing now. You were going to use force—the force of money—to make me do what you wanted. Now I'm using force to stop it. [*He levels the revolver again.*]

JAMES. You're—you're going to shoot your old uncle?

PHILIP. Why not? I've shot lots of old uncles—Landsturmers.

JAMES. But those were Germans! It's different shooting

Germans. You're in England now. You couldn't have a crime on your conscience like that.

PHILIP. Ah, but you mustn't think that after four years of war one has quite the same ideas about the sanctity of human life. How could one?

JAMES. You'll find that juries have kept pretty much the same ideas, I fancy.

PHILIP. Yes, but revolvers often go off accidentally. You said so yourself. This is going to be the purest accident. Can't you see it in the papers? "The deceased's nephew, who was obviously upset——"

JAMES. I suppose you think it's brave to come back from the front and threaten a defenceless man with a revolver? Is that the sort of fair play they teach you in the Army?

PHILIP. Good heavens! of course it is. You don't think that you wait until the other side has got just as many guns as you before you attack? You're really rather lucky. Strictly speaking, I ought to have thrown half a dozen bombs at you first. [*Taking one out of his pocket*] As it happens, I've only got one.

JAMES [*thoroughly alarmed*]. Put that back at once.

PHILIP [*putting down the revolver and taking it in his hands*]. You hold it in the right hand—so—taking care to keep the lever down. Then you take the pin in the finger—so, and—but perhaps this doesn't interest you?

JAMES [*edging his chair away*]. Put it down at once, sir. Good heavens! anything might happen.

PHILIP [*putting it down and taking up the revolver again*]. Does it ever occur to you, Uncle James, that there are about three million people in England who know all about bombs, and how to throw them, and——

JAMES. It certainly does not occur to me. I should never dream of letting these things occur to me.

THE BOY COMES HOME

PHILIP [*looking at the bomb regretfully*]. It's rather against my principles as a soldier, but just to make things a bit more fair—[*generously*] you shall have it. [*He holds it out to him suddenly.*]

JAMES [*shrinking back again*]. Certainly not, sir. It might go off at any moment.

PHILIP [*putting it back in his pocket*]. Oh no; it's quite useless; there's no detonator. . . . [*Sternly*] Now, then, let's talk business.

JAMES. What do you want me to do?

PHILIP. Strictly speaking, you should be holding your hands over your head and saying "Kamerad!" However, I'll let you off that. All I ask from you is that you should be reasonable.

JAMES. And if I refuse, you'll shoot me?

PHILIP. Well, I don't quite know, Uncle James. I expect we should go through this little scene again to-morrow. You haven't enjoyed it, have you? Well, there's lots more of it to come. We'll rehearse it every day. One day, if you go on being unreasonable, the thing will go off. Of course, you think that I shouldn't have the pluck to fire. But you can't be quite certain. It's a hundred to one that I shan't—only I might. Fear—it's a horrible thing. Elderly men die of it sometimes.

JAMES. Pooh! I'm not to be bluffed like that.

PHILIP [*suddenly*]. You're quite right; you're not that sort. I made a mistake. [*Aiming carefully*] I shall have to do it straight off, after all. One—two——

JAMES [*on his knees, with uplifted hands, in an agony of terror*]. Philip! Mercy! What are your terms?

PHILIP [*picking him up by the scruff, and helping him into the chair*]. Good man, that's the way to talk. I'll get them for you. Make yourself comfortable in front of the fire till I come back. Here's the paper. [*He gives his uncle the paper, and goes out into the hall.*]

* * * * * *

[JAMES *opens his eyes with a start and looks round him in a bewildered way. He rubs his head, takes out his watch and looks at it, and then stares round the room again. The door from the dining-room opens, and* PHILIP *comes in with a piece of toast in his hand.*

PHILIP [*his mouth full*]. You wanted to see me, Uncle James?

JAMES [*still bewildered*]. That's all right, my boy, that's all right. What have you been doing?

PHILIP [*surprised*]. Breakfast. [*Putting the last piece in his mouth*] Rather late, I'm afraid.

JAMES. That's all right. [*He laughs awkwardly.*]

PHILIP. Anything the matter? You don't look your usual bright self.

JAMES. I—er—seem to have dropped asleep in front of the fire. Most unusual thing for me to have done. Most unusual.

PHILIP. Let that be a lesson to you not to get up so early. Of course, if you're in the Army you can't help yourself. Thank heaven I'm out of it, and my own master again.

JAMES. Ah, that's what I wanted to talk to you about. Sit down, Philip. [*He indicates the chair by the fire.*]

PHILIP [*taking a chair by the table*]. You have that, uncle; I shall be all right here.

JAMES [*hastily*]. No, no; you come here. [*He gives* PHILIP *the armchair and sits by the table himself.*] I should be dropping off again. [*He laughs awkwardly.*]

PHILIP. Righto. [*He puts his hand to his pocket.* UNCLE

THE BOY COMES HOME

JAMES *shivers and looks at him in horror.* PHILIP *brings out his pipe, and a sickly grin of relief comes into* JAMES'S *face.*]

JAMES. I suppose you smoked a lot in France?

PHILIP. Rather! Nothing else to do. It's allowed in here?

JAMES [*hastily*]. Yes, yes, of course. [PHILIP *lights his pipe.*] Well now, Philip, what are you going to do, now you've left the Army?

PHILIP [*promptly*]. Burn my uniform and sell my revolver.

JAMES [*starting at the word "revolver"*]. Sell your revolver, eh?

PHILIP [*surprised*]. Well, I don't want it now, do I?

JAMES. No. . . . Oh no. . . . Oh, most certainly not, I should say. Oh, I can't see why you should want it at all. [*With an uneasy laugh*] You're in England now. No need for revolvers here—eh?

PHILIP [*staring at him*]. Well, no, I hope not.

JAMES [*hastily*]. Quite so. Well now, Philip, what next? We must find a profession for you.

PHILIP [*yawning*]. I suppose so. I haven't really thought about it much.

JAMES. You never wanted to be an architect?

PHILIP [*surprised*]. Architect? [JAMES *rubs his head and wonders what made him think of architect.*]

JAMES. Or anything like that.

PHILIP. It's a bit late, isn't it?

JAMES. Well, if you're four years behind, so is everybody else. [*He feels vaguely that he has heard this argument before.*]

PHILIP [*smiling*]. To tell the truth, I don't feel I mind much anyway. Anything you like—except a commissionaire. I absolutely refuse to wear uniform again.

JAMES. How would you like to come into the business?

PHILIP. The jam business? Well, I don't know. You wouldn't want me to salute you in the mornings?

JAMES. My dear boy, no!

PHILIP. All right, I'll try it if you like. I don't know if I shall be any good—what do you do?

JAMES. It's your experience in managing and—er—handling men which I hope will be of value.

PHILIP. Oh, I can do that all right. [*Stretching himself luxuriously*] Uncle James, do you realize that I'm never going to salute again, or wear a uniform, or get wet—really wet, I mean—or examine men's feet, or stand to attention when I'm spoken to, or—oh, lots more things? And best of all, I'm never going to be frightened again. Have you ever known what it is to be afraid—really afraid?

JAMES [*embarrassed*]. I—er—well—— [*He coughs.*]

PHILIP. No, you couldn't—not really afraid of death, I mean. Well, that's over now. Good lord! I could spend the rest of my life in the British Museum and be happy. . . .

JAMES [*getting up*]. All right, we'll try you in the office. I expect you want a holiday first, though.

PHILIP [*getting up*]. My dear uncle, this is holiday. Being in London is holiday. Buying an evening paper—wearing a waistcoat again—running after a bus—anything—it's all holiday.

JAMES. All right, then, come along with me now, and I'll introduce you to Mr Bamford.

PHILIP. Right. Who's he?

JAMES. Our manager. A little stiff, but a very good fellow. He'll be delighted to hear that you are coming into the firm.

PHILIP [*smiling*]. Perhaps I'd better bring my revolver, in case he isn't.

THE BOY COMES HOME

JAMES [*laughing with forced heartiness as they go together to the door*]. Ha, ha! A good joke that! Ha, ha, ha! A good joke—but only a joke, of course. Ha, ha! He, he, he!

> [PHILIP *goes out.* JAMES, *following him, turns at the door, and looks round the room in a bewildered way. Was it a dream, or wasn't it? He will never be quite certain.*

CURTAIN

Applications regarding amateur performances of this play should be addressed to Messrs Samuel French, Ltd., 26 Southampton Street, Strand, London, W.C.2, or 28–30 West 38th Street, New York.

FOLLOWERS
A "CRANFORD" SKETCH
By Harold Brighouse

Mr Harold Brighouse began by writing Lancashire plays, and naturally belonged to the Manchester school of drama. He has a long list of plays to his credit, but the best are undoubtedly "The Odd Man Out," "Garside's Career," and "Hobson's Choice." The last play brought him fame, for it had a great success on both sides of the Atlantic and in most of the countries of Europe.

Mr Brighouse is primarily interested in people. He can tell a good story and construct a delightful plot, but one feels that he is most fascinated by human nature and aims always at making his characters live. It is for this reason, perhaps, that the plays act even better than they read.

His one-act plays, such as "Lonesome-like," "The Price of Coal," and "Maid of France" are excellent, and reveal great versatility. He is continually experimenting, and it is a great mistake to regard him solely as a writer of Lancashire comedies. Like Mr A. A. Milne, Mr Brighouse is still young, and his best work may still be unwritten. During the last few years he has been writing novels, and has already established himself as an author as well as a playwright.

CHARACTERS

LUCINDA BAINES
HELEN MASTERS
SUSAN CROWTHER
COLONEL REDFERN

This play was first produced by Mr Milton Rosmer's Repertory Company at the Princes' Theatre, Manchester, on Monday, April 12, 1915, with the following cast:

Lucinda Baines .	. IRENE ROOKE
Helen Masters .	. DOROTHY RIPLEY
Susan Crowther .	. EVELYN MARTHEGE
Colonel Redfern .	. F. RANDLE AYRTON

Mrs Gaskell is an excellent author to steal from, but, though her novels are equally a possession of us all, a dramatic common or open space where every dramatist has rights, *Cranford* offers perhaps the least promising field for stage adaptation. The theatre is a terribly downright place, and the subtleties of the stage are the platitudes of life. It was therefore purely in an experimental spirit that I set out to see whether the fragile delicacy of *Cranford* could be translated with any measure of success into terms of the stage. I began by taking a story which very well might have been, and almost was, in *Cranford*, and I pretended that my little town was not Mrs Gaskell's "Cranford," but a neighbouring place rather like it. People read the result and said, "But this is *Cranford*"—which was precisely what I dared to hope they might say. It seemed to hint success. But there remained the stage, the only test for any play. Books are their authors', but, in the making of a play, author, producer, actors, and audience must all collaborate, and it is wise, in addition, to engage a good fairy to watch over the birth of one's play. "Followers" happened to be lucky. Miss Irene Rooke is an actress of genius; that has been said before, but truth does not stale with repetition. Her performance in "Followers" was a thing of wistful beauty, and it is first to Miss Rooke's acting, and second to Mr Milton Rosmer's skilled producing, that I owe the success which this little play achieved on the stage.

H. B.

FOLLOWERS

Scene: *The parlour of* Miss Lucinda Baines *at Cranford, in June* 1859. *It is the room of an old maid of the period, overcrowded with fragile furniture, spattered with antimacassars and china. The room is filled with the bright light of a summer's morning. Bushes and green hedge are seen through the window* C. *The door is* L.

Susan Crowther, *a ruddy country girl of twenty-two, shows in* Helen Masters, *a young lady of the same age, in summer outdoor clothes.*

Susan. Miss Baines says, will you please take a seat, Miss Masters, and she'll be down in a minute.

Helen [*not sitting*]. Susan, go at once and tell your mistress I shall be seriously offended if she has gone upstairs to change her cap on my account.

Susan [*severely*]. Miss Baines would not think of receiving a visitor without changing her cap, Miss Masters.

Helen. I am not a visitor here, and, if I am, this is an early morning call and——

Susan [*finally*]. Miss Baines is changing her cap and there's an end of it. She won't be long.

Helen [*defeated, sitting*]. Oh, I am sorry, but this was my only opportunity of seeing her. I return to London this afternoon.

Susan [*awed*]. By the train, miss?

Helen [*smiling*]. Yes.

Susan. You have more courage than I have.

Helen. Tell me, Susan, your mistress keeps well?

41

SUSAN. She's well enough. Will worry herself, you know. Solomon has been a great disappointment to her.

HELEN. Solomon? Who is Solomon?

SUSAN. Solomon is the cat. He had kittens, and the shock nearly sent Miss Baines to her bed.

HELEN. Oh, dear!

SUSAN. We still call her Solomon because she's used to it, but things will never be the same again. Miss Baines feels that Solomon has deceived her.

HELEN. And you, Susan?

SUSAN. Oh, I am quite well. Miss—[*pausing awkwardly, then*]—Miss Masters!

HELEN. Yes. Nothing wrong?

SUSAN. No, but—Miss Masters—you are one the mistress listens to. She's—there is one thing that sorely troubles me, and, if you would speak a word for me, I'm sure——

HELEN. What is it, Susan?

SUSAN. Well, miss, when I came here ten years ago—straight from the Charity School it was—Miss Baines said when she took me, "Now, Susan, no followers," she said, and I said, "No, mem, never." I passed my word when I was too young to know, and there's many wouldn't keep it on that account, but——

HELEN. Do you want followers, Susan?

SUSAN. No, miss, I don't. Not followers. One follower at a time's enough for any woman.

HELEN. You've somebody in mind?

SUSAN. I've seen James Brown look at me and I wouldn't say if it wasn't for my promise but that James——

HELEN. I see.

SUSAN. But I promised and I'm not the one to break my word, only when I try to put it to the mistress it's as if she saw it coming, and there's something in her eye that stops me asking. And it's not as if she never had a follower herself.

FOLLOWERS

HELEN [*rising*]. Susan!

SUSAN [*defending herself*]. A body can't live ten years in Cranford without hearing that old story of Miss Baines and———

HELEN. Hush, Susan.

SUSAN. Well, it's true, and, what's more, he's back from India now. I've seen him.

HELEN. Mr Redfern is back?

SUSAN. You spoke his name, not I. Yes, he's back.

HELEN. When?

SUSAN. I only know I was carrying the basket yesterday while Miss Baines bought the grocery in Mr Wilson's shop, and there was a gentleman inside when we went in, buying matches to light his cheroot———

HELEN. A cheroot in Cranford High Street!

SUSAN. Yes, miss, and he raised his hat to Miss Baines, and she gave a jump and held my arm hard, and just said, " Mr Redfern "—gasping, like that—" Mr Redfern," and went on giving her orders as if nothing had happened. She's a brave woman, though I say it that's her own servant. And, if she had him once, why mayn't I have James Brown?

HELEN. I will see what I can do, Susan.

> [*Enter* LUCINDA. *She is a fragile old maid of fifty, delicate in her dress, with transparent complexion, grey clothes, and lace cap.*

LUCINDA. Helen!

HELEN. Dear Miss Baines.   [*They kiss. Exit* SUSAN. Pardon this early call.

LUCINDA. You could not come too early, Helen.

[*They sit.*

HELEN. This was my only chance. I arrived yesterday and return to-day.

LUCINDA. Cranford will not see much of you now.

HELEN. Now?

LUCINDA. I have heard the great news, Helen. You are betrothed.

HELEN. Yes, Miss Baines. [*Pause.*] You do not wish me joy.

LUCINDA. Child, I have always wished you every joy.

HELEN. I want you to know Harry, Miss Baines. He is here with me, but I know no gentleman has entered your house as long as I remember, yet I hoped you might make an exception in my case.

LUCINDA. Helen, you are not asking me to receive your affianced husband in this house?

HELEN. Forgive the recklessness of my desire. I have so great a wish that Harry should see this room where you taught me to work my samplers and to knit.

LUCINDA. I should take great pleasure in seeing him if I could meet him out. Here, as you know, I have no apartment suited for the entertainment of a gentleman. I should be in agonies for the safety of my china. I was for long uneasy about Solomon until I found that cats tread with the most prudent delicacy. But men's movements are singularly lacking in grace.

HELEN. Harry is very gentle.

LUCINDA. Without doubt, my dear. But a man is so much in the way in a house. He must himself feel out of place.

HELEN [*smiling*]. Would you have them live in the stables?

LUCINDA. I make no rule for others, Helen. For myself, I am quite decided.

HELEN. And for Susan too?

LUCINDA. Susan, my dear?

HELEN. Susan is in love, but she will not break the promise made to you.

FOLLOWERS

LUCINDA. My dear, I said, " No followers," and I meant no followers. If Susan is in love she has her fortnightly evening, and I am broad-minded enough not to ask too closely with whom she walks to the Dorcas Meeting, but my kitchen is no place for Susan's sweetheart. Men of our own order speak habitually in voices too loud for a room, let alone one of Susan's class.

HELEN [*pleading*]. She finds it lonely, I am afraid.

LUCINDA. Susan has her work.

HELEN. Do you never feel lonely here in the dark winter evenings?

LUCINDA. Lonely, child? I used to be afraid of loneliness, and once, when there had been some burglaries in Cranford, I did think how much safer I should have felt with a husband by my side. . . . Does it shock you to hear me talk of husbands?

HELEN. No, no. I try not to speak the word myself, because I know that one should not before the time, but it cannot really be immodest.

LUCINDA. Yes, I remember the time when I looked forward to being married as much as anyone, but the person I once thought I might be married to went far away because I said " No " when I didn't mean it, only he thought I did, and I don't know to this day why I did say " No " when all of me was throbbing to say " Yes." Oh, Helen, Helen, be very happy with your Harry. Thank God *you* did not say " No."

HELEN. I hope I am a modest woman, Miss Baines. I said " No " twice, but Harry asked three times, and at the third I thought it became me to yield.

LUCINDA. Mr Redfern asked but once and then he went away.

HELEN. Mr Redfern!

LUCINDA. That was his name. I did not mean to mention

it. Pray forget I did so, Helen. Old memories are best forgotten.

HELEN. Mr Redfern. But . . . Miss Baines . . . there is still the future.

LUCINDA. No, there are ghosts of the past that are hard to lay, but for me there is no future. I have lived so long with my shadows that I should fear the light.

HELEN. Your shadows?

LUCINDA. Oh, you will not come to live in the shadow-world. There in the light your husband and your children are waiting and calling for you to come.

HELEN. You make me feel ashamed.

LUCINDA. Ashamed? Whatever for? Be proud of life and joy.

HELEN. I have so much. I want so much and you are contented with so little.

LUCINDA. I? Life is for the young, life and the golden day. For me, age and the shadows. Yes, Helen, I used to be afraid of loneliness. I used to weep because the days were long and the nights were longer still.

HELEN. And now?

LUCINDA. Now I have the children of my dreams. They are just like other people's children, Helen, only mine are all, all my own. They don't grow up. They don't grow big and clumsy. They are always small and neat, and beautiful and well behaved. They come to me when I am alone, and then, you see, I am not alone. They sit upon those seats that I keep near the fire, so that in winter they can watch the glow—that is Mary's, and the little hassock there is John's—and their boots are never dirty, and they don't disturb the antimacassars, and their voices are soft and low. And in the night I have wakened with the clasp of their arms about my neck, and my darlings put up their little mouths to mine to be kissed just as I've seen real babies do to real mothers.

HELEN. I wonder if it is better so.

LUCINDA [*with energy*]. No, no. Never. Forget this, Helen. I have spoken things I did not mean to speak. Tell me more of your betrothal. Is your trousseau far advanced? You must have lavender from my garden. Lavender for one's dresses and rose-leaves for one's rooms. And I have both for you.

Enter SUSAN

SUSAN [*awkwardly*]. Miss Baines.

LUCINDA. What is it, Susan?

SUSAN. There's a gentleman at the door, and he is asking for you.

LUCINDA. A gentleman!

SUSAN [*volubly*]. Oh, Miss Baines, if you please, it's the gentleman we saw yesterday in Mr Wilson's shop, only he is dressed grander still to-day. I told him you couldn't see him, but I might as well have talked at the wall of a house.

LUCINDA [*pauses, then collects her courage*]. I will see him, Susan, please.

SUSAN [*staggered*]. In here?

LUCINDA. Yes.

SUSAN. Save us, what goings-on! [*Exit* SUSAN.

LUCINDA. Helen, stand by me. This is my hour of trial. Don't leave me, child.

HELEN. Not if you wish me to remain.

LUCINDA. My courage is not all I could desire. Thank God you are here, Helen. It's a mercy you came and I changed my cap for you.

HELEN. You're looking splendid, dear; you have a colour.

LUCINDA. I am all of a twitter. Is my cap straight?

HELEN. You are perfect.

LUCINDA. Helen, what should I offer him? Do gentlemen take gooseberry wine? Do they drink tea in the morning? I don't know anything. I am so ignorant of men.

HELEN. He will not want anything but you.

> [*Enter* SUSAN, *smirking, and* CHARLES REDFERN. *Exit* SUSAN *without announcing*. REDFERN *is a spare, soldierly figure of fifty-five, grey-haired, very brown, dressed carefully. He is shy, talking at one moment as if addressing a squad, then, remembering, is subdued for a time before resuming his usual commanding tone.*

LUCINDA [*bowing*]. Mr Redfern.

REDFERN [*bowing*]. Colonel, madam, colonel, retired from the service of the East India Company.

LUCINDA [*introducing*]. Colonel Redfern. My god-daughter, Miss Masters. [*They bow.*

REDFERN. Your servant, madam.

LUCINDA. Will you sit down, Colonel? [REDFERN *looks doubtfully.*] . . . Er . . . That chair is stronger than it looks. I think you have no cause for apprehension.

REDFERN [*sitting*]. I thank you, madam. [*It is a very low chair and his long legs make him acutely conscious of it.*]

LUCINDA. May I offer you refreshment, Colonel? A little gooseberry wine, or——

REDFERN. I thank you, no. I do not like gooseberries. [*He looks at* HELEN, *resenting her presence. Pause.*]

LUCINDA [*embarrassed but brave*]. You must find Cranford a dull place after your martial career, Colonel Redfern.

REDFERN. I find it very pleasant to be back in England.

LUCINDA. It is safer, I have no doubt. Did you find the Asiatics very fierce?

REDFERN [*glancing at* HELEN]. I have not come here to talk about myself, Miss Baines.

FOLLOWERS

LUCINDA. But yours has been an adventurous life. Surely——

REDFERN. Pardon me, madam, a soldier's tales are not for a lady's ear. My life is of less interest to you than yours is to me.

LUCINDA. Mine! But I——

REDFERN [*rising*]. Yes. That is what I have come to hear, and as Miss Masters is your god-daughter she must know all about you, and I fear it would only weary her to hear you telling me.

LUCINDA. I am sure Helen will not mind. I have nothing to tell.

HELEN [*rising*]. Yes, Colonel Redfern, I ought to leave you two old friends together.

LUCINDA [*rising, frightened*]. But, Helen! Colonel, your arrival interrupted us. Helen was telling me of her betrothal.

REDFERN [*bowing*]. I congratulate Miss Masters.

HELEN. Thank you, Colonel Redfern.

LUCINDA. Go on, Helen.

HELEN. Really, Miss Baines, there is nothing more to tell.

REDFERN. Ah! And so?

HELEN. May I have a word with Susan before I go?

LUCINDA. You are not going!

HELEN. I must.

LUCINDA. But——

HELEN. I will step in later on to say farewell. Good morning, Colonel Redfern.

REDFERN [*opening door and bowing*]. Good morning, Miss Masters [*as she passes him*], and bless you for a sensible girl.

[*Exit* HELEN. *He turns from closing the door and speaks commandingly.*

Now, Lucy.

LUCINDA [*faintly protesting*]. Colonel Redfern!

REDFERN. I remind you, Lucy, that my Christian name is Charles.

LUCINDA. I had not forgotten.

REDFERN. Nor the last time you called me by it, I warrant. This very room, wasn't it? I never had such a downfall in my life. In I came, found you alone, popped the question, and when you rapped out your "No" I could have dropped through the floor for simple wonderment, I'd made so sure you were only waiting to be asked. I've taken some gruelling in my time, but I was never harder hit than on that day—how many?—twenty-five years ago?

LUCINDA. Twenty-five years, three months, ten days. It was March seventeenth, 1834.

REDFERN. Ah? So you've not forgotten. No, nor I. Nor the way I cut and ran like a whipped dog with my tail between my legs—all the way to India as fast as sail and wind would carry me. And, do you know, Lucy, I've been trying ever since the day I landed there to get home again. For twenty-five years I've been trying. That's why I never wrote. I always expected myself to be here as quickly as a letter. At first I couldn't get leave, and if I had I couldn't have paid my passage, and when I got leave I had fever, and when I recovered from the fever I'd to go on active service—and when I was better from my wound——

LUCINDA. You were wounded!

REDFERN. A trifle that time, but it kept me there till the next affair, and so it's gone on all these years till the Mutiny came, and I went through that without a scratch, and thought it time to send my papers in and make for home. And that's the last word I'll say about myself. Now, Lucy, what have you been doing?

LUCINDA. I? Living at home.

FOLLOWERS

REDFERN. Do you know what home means to me? I used to hear the other fellows talk of home—mothers, sisters, sweethearts, wives, and children. Home meant something to us all. It meant Cranford to me.

LUCINDA. But you hadn't used to live in Cranford.

REDFERN. You did, and Cranford meant you. Lucy, don't you know why I have come home?

LUCINDA. Have you not reached the age for retirement?

REDFERN. Age? I am as young as on the day I went away. I've come to ask you a question, Lucy. It's the doubt that lay heavy on my mind the day I landed in India, and made me want to take the next ship home, and it's not grown less since then. It's this—suppose I hadn't listened to you, suppose I had asked again, would you still have told me " No "?

LUCINDA. How can I tell what I should have said?

REDFERN. Come, Lucy, you had the date off pat. You'd not forgotten that.

LUCINDA. It is all so many years ago.

REDFERN. You mean I am to let bygones be bygones.

LUCINDA. If you please, Colonel Redfern.

REDFERN. No, madam, I do not please. But I obey. The past is past—but there remains the future.

LUCINDA. Are you going to make your future home in Cranford, Colonel?

REDFERN. I hope so, Lucy. I shall stay on at the George until I've looked round, and then, I trust, anchorage.

LUCINDA. Then no doubt we shall have friends in common at whose houses we may chance to meet sometimes.

REDFERN. Other people's houses! You're a cordial hostess, Lucy.

LUCINDA. Colonel Redfern, you have recalled the occasion when last you visited me. My father was already dead, and, since the day of your call, no gentleman has entered my house until to-day. Your coming here breaks all my rules.

REDFERN. Then I think it's time you had a little male society.

LUCINDA. This is an old maid's house.

REDFERN. Old maid be hanged. I beg your pardon, Lucy. A soldier's bluntness. But I am seeing you now as I saw you then with your bonny face and those dear blue eyes with what I fancied was the love-light in them, though now I know that it was just the sunshine of your soul, and the smile that has made my fever-bed a thing of joy because I could lie still and think of you and—and—yes, madam, I will say it—the neatest ankle in the world peeping out below your petticoats. The Lord forgive me for recalling such a thing, but you wouldn't believe the comfort that ankle's been to me in India.

LUCINDA. Colonel, hadn't you better rub your eyes?

REDFERN. Why, madam?

LUCINDA. To see me as I am.

REDFERN. I see no change. It might have been yesterday.

LUCINDA. You are laughing at me.

REDFERN. I do not laugh at my divinity.

LUCINDA. Then it is your pleasure, sir, to be gallant, and I suggest you find a better subject for your gallantry than a lean and wrinkled——

REDFERN. Lucy, have you a looking-glass?

LUCINDA. I see my wrinkles in it every day.

REDFERN. Your glass tells lies.

LUCINDA. Colonel, I am too old for compliments. May I ask you to state what is the object of your visit?

REDFERN. The object, madam! Upon my word, you are a little short.

LUCINDA. I find you, sir, a little long.

FOLLOWERS

REDFERN. Very well, madam, I will be brief. It is not the custom of the Service to beat about the bush. I have an object, and the object is to ask you to be my wife. It's the second time of asking, Lucy, and it's a plaguey long time since the first, but that was not my fault. It's the lady's privilege to change her mind. Won't you change yours?

LUCINDA. Yes, Charles, my mind is changed.

REDFERN [*approaching gladly*]. Lucy?

LUCINDA [*backing with hand up*]. You do not understand.

REDFERN. I understand that you have changed your mind, and——

LUCINDA. Charles, when I said " No," it was my lips that spoke. My mind, my heart were aching to say " Yes "— five-and-twenty years ago. To-day I am all united when I answer " No."

REDFERN. Ah, but I'll not take " No " this time. I'll ask and ask again until——

LUCINDA. Till what, Charles? Till I become a girl again? Your asking will not bring back my youth, nor yours.

REDFERN. Mine? Time does not matter if love keeps young.

LUCINDA. Has yours kept young?

REDFERN. It is young and fresh and strong as on the day I went away. It's never flagged. It's——

LUCINDA. And I will tell you why. Because you went away and had a great career in India. You put your love aside and filled your mind with other thoughts.

REDFERN. Not filled.

LUCINDA. Oh, sparing me a small recess, securely sealed, as I seal up my autumn plums. You took it out sometimes, that thought of me, to polish up and put it back in its recess until the next campaign was over and gave you leisure for another look. But I'd no splendid wars to occupy my mind. I had no seal to put upon my love to keep it fresh. The pain was great until Time came to heal the open sore. Time put a halo round your love for me, but Time killed mine for you.

REDFERN. Lucy, it is not too late. Love doesn't die. It sleeps. Let me awaken yours to life.

LUCINDA. It has been too late for many years. Charles, I want you to understand. It is too late. I do not look for happiness. I have contentment.

REDFERN. And what have I?

LUCINDA. You have had your life, a full life, Charles, a man's life.

REDFERN. I have lived on hopes. I can't live on regrets.

LUCINDA. Change them to memories.

REDFERN. Of what?

LUCINDA. Of what? For you the years have brought a great career. For me catastrophe.

REDFERN. Then—then is there no hope for me, Lucy?

LUCINDA. None.

REDFERN [*moving towards door*]. In India, I have not known defeat.

LUCINDA. You are back in England now, Colonel.

REDFERN. Colonel!

LUCINDA [*extending hand*]. Good-bye, Charles.

REDFERN [*taking it, appealingly*]. Lucy! [*She shakes her head.*] Good-bye.

> [*Exit* REDFERN. LUCY *sits, opens the locket she wears on a chain round her neck and buries it against her face, kissing it.*

Enter HELEN, *softly*

HELEN. May I come in?

FOLLOWERS

LUCINDA [*closing locket*]. Helen, did I disappoint you greatly when I said I could not receive your Harry?

HELEN. We both hoped very much that he might come.

LUCINDA. Helen, tell him from me that he may come, just once, if he will wipe his boots most carefully and sit there quietly in the centre of the room.

HELEN. Oh, thank you, Miss Baines. You can't tell how much pleasure you will give us both.

[*Exit* HELEN. MISS BAINES *carefully straightens her antimacassars.* SUSAN *knocks.*

LUCINDA. Come in. [SUSAN *enters.*

SUSAN [*awed*]. Miss Baines!

LUCINDA. What is it, Susan?

SUSAN. The gentleman.

LUCINDA. Yes?

SUSAN. He gave me this [*showing sovereign*]. Am I to keep it, mem?

LUCINDA. Certainly, Susan.

SUSAN. He said it was for a new gown or—or a present for my sweetheart and—oh, miss, I do not want a gown, and I do so want a sweetheart, and I don't care if it is forward to say it, for I do.

LUCINDA. You remember I said " No followers," Susan.

SUSAN. Yes, miss, I have not forgotten, nor likely to, neither.

LUCINDA. You are young, Susan.

SUSAN. Not me. I'm twenty-three in November.

LUCINDA. Yes, you're young.

SUSAN. Too young for a sweetheart, miss?

LUCINDA. No, Susan. I did say you were to have no followers, but if you meet with a man you like and let me know, and I find on proper inquiry that he is respectable, I shall have no objection to his coming to see you once a week, if he will promise to move carefully in the kitchen and abstain from raising his voice.

SUSAN [*kneeling at Lucinda's feet*]. Oh, Miss Baines!

LUCINDA [*simply*]. God forbid that I should grieve any young hearts.

CURTAIN

Inquiries respecting the acting rights in this play should be addressed to the author's agent, Miss Elisabeth Marbury 20 Queen Street, Leicester Square, London, W.C.2, or to the American Play Company, Inc., 33 West 42nd Street, New York.

For amateur performances the agents are Messrs Samuel French, Ltd., 26 Southampton Street, Strand, London, W.C.2, and 28–30 West 38th Street, New York.

THE STEPMOTHER
A FARCE IN ONE ACT

By Arnold Bennett

Mr Arnold Bennett's best plays are "Milestones" (written in collaboration with Mr Edward Knoblock), "The Great Adventure," and "What the Public Wants." There are others, of course, but the three indicated are pre-eminent. A one-act play like "The Stepmother" shows his genius, but it does him less than justice. It was written when he was thirty-two.

Mr Arnold Bennett appeals to the public as a novelist first and a dramatist second, whereas we have come to regard Mr Galsworthy as a dramatist first and a novelist second. The idea may be wrong, but it undoubtedly exists. Mr Bennett's best novels are generally held to be *The Old Wives' Tale*, *Riceyman Steps*, and the *Clayhanger* trilogy.

Both in fiction and in drama he excels in amusing comedy with a strong flavour of satire. His influence is entirely healthy. He is famous for his minute knowledge of human nature and for his skill in laying bare all that is best and worst in the characters he describes.

CHARACTERS

CORA PROUT, *a popular novelist and a widow, aged thirty*
ADRIAN PROUT, *her stepson, aged twenty*
THOMAS GARDNER, *a doctor, aged thirty-five*
CHRISTINE FEVERSHAM, *Mrs Prout's secretary, aged twenty*

"The Stepmother" has not been produced professionally.

THE STEPMOTHER

SCENE: MRS PROUT's *study: luxuriously furnished; large table in centre, upon which are a new novel, Press-cuttings, and the usual apparatus of literary compositions.* CHRISTINE *is seated at the large table, ready for work, and awaiting the advent of* MRS PROUT. *To pass the time she picks up the novel, the leaves of which are not cut, and glances at a page here and there. Enter* MRS PROUT, *hurried and preoccupied; the famous novelist is attired in a plain morning gown, which in the perfection of its cut displays the beauty of her figure. She nods absently to* CHRISTINE, *and sits down in an armchair away from the table.*

CHRISTINE. Good morning, Mrs Prout. I'm afraid you are still sleeping badly.

MRS PROUT. Do I look it, girl?

CHRISTINE. You don't specially look it, Mrs Prout. But I observe. You are my third novelist, and they have all taught me to observe. Before I took up novelists I was with a Member of Parliament, and he never observed anything except five-line whips.

MRS PROUT. Really! Five-line whips! Oblige me by putting that down in Notebook No. 2. There will be an M.P. in that wretched thirty-thousand-word thing I've promised for the Christmas number of the *New York Surpriser* and it might be useful. I might even make an epigram out of it.

CHRISTINE. Yes, Mrs Prout. [*Writes.*]

MRS PROUT. And what are your observations about me?

CHRISTINE [*while writing*]. Well, this is twice in three weeks that you've been here five minutes late in the morning.

MRS PROUT. Is that all? You don't think my stuff's falling off?

CHRISTINE. Oh, *no*, Mrs Prout! I *know* it's not falling off. I was just going to tell you. The butler's been in, and wished me to inform you that he begged to give notice. [*Looking up*] It seems that last night you ordered him to cut the leaves of our new novel. [*Patting book maternally*] He said he just looked into it, and he thinks it's disgraceful to ask a respectable butler to cut the leaves of such a book. So he begs to give warning. Oh, no, Mrs Prout, your stuff isn't falling off.

MRS PROUT [*grimly*]. What did you say to him, girl?

CHRISTINE. First I looked at him, and then I said, " Brown, you will probably be able to get a place on the reviewing staff of the *Methodist Recorder*."

MRS PROUT. Christine, one day, I really believe, you will come to employ a secretary of your own.

CHRISTINE. I hope so, Mrs Prout. But I intend to keep off the morbid introspection line. *You* do that so awfully well. I think I shall go in for smart dialogue, with marquises and country houses, and a touch of old-fashioned human nature at the bottom. It appears to me that's what's coming along very shortly. . . . Shall we begin, Mrs Prout?

MRS PROUT [*disinclined*]. Yes, I suppose so. [*Clearing her throat*] By the way, anything special in the Press-cuttings?

CHRISTINE. Nothing very special. [*Fingering the pile of Press-cuttings*] The *Morning Call* says, " genius in every line."

THE STEPMOTHER

MRS PROUT [*blasé*]. Hum!

CHRISTINE. The *Daily Reporter* : " Cora Prout may be talented—we should hesitate to deny it—but she is one of several of our leading novelists who should send themselves to a Board School in order to learn grammar."

MRS PROUT. Grammar again! They must keep a grammar in the office! Personally I think it's frightfully bad form to talk about grammar to a lady. But they never had any taste at the *Reporter*. Don't read me any more. Let us commence work.

CHRISTINE. Which will you do, Mrs Prout ? [*Consulting a diary of engagements*] There's the short story for the *Illustrated Monthly*, six thousand, promised for next Saturday. There's the article on " Women's Diversions " for the *British Review*—they wrote for that yesterday. There's the serial that begins in the *Sunday Daily Sentinel* in September—you've only done half the first instalment of that. And of course there's *Heart Ache*.

MRS PROUT. I think I'll go on with *Heart Ache*. I feel it coming. I'll do the short story for the *Illustrated* to-morrow. Where had I got to?

CHRISTINE [*choosing the correct notebook reads*]. " The inanimate form of the patient lay like marble on the marble slab of the operating table. ' The sponge, Nurse,' said the doctor, ' where is it ? ' " That's where you'd got to.

MRS PROUT. Yes. I remember. New line. " Isabel gazed at him imperturbably." New line. Quote-marks. " ' I fear, Doctor,' she remarked, ' that in a moment of forgetfulness you have sewn it up in our poor patient.' " New line. Quote-marks. " ' Damn ! ' said the doctor, ' so I have.' " Rather good, that, Christine, eh ?

[CHRISTINE *writes in shorthand*.

CHRISTINE. Oh, Mrs Prout, I think it's beautiful. So staccato and crisp. By the way, I forgot to tell you that there's a leader in the *Daily Snail* on that frightful anonymous attack in the *Forum* against your medical accuracy. [*Looking at* MRS PROUT, *who is silent, but shows signs of agitation*] You remember—" Medicine in Fiction." The *Snail* backs up the *Forum* for all it's worth. . . . Mrs Prout, you *are* ill. I was sure you were. What can I get for you ?

MRS PROUT [*weakly wiping her eyes*]. Nonsense, Christine. I am a little unstrung, that is all. I want nothing.

CHRISTINE. Your imagination is too much for you.

MRS PROUT [*meekly*]. Perhaps so.

CHRISTINE [*firmly*]. But it isn't all due to an abnormal imagination. You've never been quite cheerful since you turned Mr Adrian out.

MRS PROUT. You forget yourself, Christine.

CHRISTINE. I forget nothing, Mrs Prout, myself least of all. Mr Adrian is your dead husband's son, and you turned him out of your house, and now you're sorry.

MRS PROUT. Christine, you know perfectly well that I—er—requested him to go because he would insist on making love to you, which interfered with our work. Besides, it was not quite nice for a man to make love to the secretary of his stepmother. I wonder you are indelicate enough to refer to the matter. You should never have permitted his advances.

CHRISTINE. I didn't permit them. I wasn't asked to. I tolerated them. I hadn't been secretary to a lady novelist with a stepson before, and I wasn't quite sure what was included in the duties. I always like to give satisfaction.

MRS PROUT. You do give satisfaction. Let that end the discussion.

CHRISTINE. [*Pouting, turning to her notebook, reads.*] "'Damn!' said the doctor, 'so I have.'" [*Pause.*] "'Damn!' said the doctor, 'so I have.'" [*Pause.*

THE STEPMOTHER

MRS PROUT. Christine, did you find out who was the author of that article on " Medicine in Fiction " ?

CHRISTINE. Is *that* what's bothering you, Mrs Prout ? Of course it was a nasty attack, but it is very unlike you to trouble about critics.

MRS PROUT. It has hurt me more than I can say. That was why I asked you to make a few discreet inquiries.

CHRISTINE. I did ask at my club.

MRS PROUT. And what did they think there ?

CHRISTINE. They laughed at me, and said every one knew you had written it yourself just to keep the silly season alive, July being a sickly month for reputations.

MRS PROUT. What did you say to that ?

CHRISTINE. I should prefer not to repeat it.

MRS PROUT. Christine, I insist. Your modesty is becoming a disease.

CHRISTINE. I said they were fools——

MRS PROUT. A little abrupt, perhaps, but effective.

CHRISTINE. Not to see that the grammar was different from ours.

MRS PROUT. Oh ! that was what you said, was it ?

CHRISTINE. It was, and it settled them.

MRS PROUT [*assuming a confidential air*]. Christine, I believe I know who wrote that article.

CHRISTINE. Who ?

MRS PROUT. Dr Gardner. [*Bursts into tears.*]

CHRISTINE [*soothing her*]. But he lives on the floor below, in the very flat underneath this.

MRS PROUT [*choking back her sobs*]. Yes. It is too dreadful.

CHRISTINE. But he comes here nearly every evening.

MRS PROUT [*sharply*]. Who told you that ?

CHRISTINE. Now, Mrs Prout, let me implore you to be calm. The butler told me. I didn't ask him, and as I cannot be expected to foretell what my employer's butler will say before he opens his mouth, I am not to blame. [*Compresses her lips.*] Shall we continue?

MRS PROUT. Christine, do you think it was Dr Gardner? I would give worlds to know.

CHRISTINE [*coldly analytic*]. Do you mean that you would give worlds to know that it was Dr Gardner, or that it wasn't Dr Gardner? Or would give worlds merely to know the author's name—no matter who he might be?

MRS PROUT [*sighing*]. You are dreadfully unsympathetic this morning.

CHRISTINE. I am placid, nothing else. Please recollect that when you engaged me you asked if you might rely on me to be placid, as your previous secretary, when you dictated the pathetic chapters, had wept so freely into her notebook that she couldn't transcribe her stuff, besides permanently injuring her eyesight. Since you ask my opinion as to Dr Gardner being the author of this attack on you, I say that he isn't. Apart from the facts that he lives on the floor below, and that he is, so the butler says, a constant visitor in the evenings, there is the additional fact—a fact which I have several times observed for myself without the assistance of the butler—that he likes you.

MRS PROUT. You **have** noticed that. It is true. But the question is: Does he like me sufficiently not to attack my work in the public Press? That is the point. The writer of that cruel article begins by saying that he has no personal animus, and that he is actuated solely by an enthusiasm for the cause of medicine and the medical profession.

CHRISTINE. You mean to infer, Mrs Prout, that the author of the article might, as a man, like you, while as a doctor he despised you?

MRS PROUT [*whimpering again*]. That is my suspicion.

THE STEPMOTHER

CHRISTINE. But Dr Gardner does more than like you. He adores you.

MRS PROUT. He adores my talent, my genius, my fame, my wealth; but does he adore me? I am not an ordinary woman, and it is no use pretending that I am. I must think of these things.

CHRISTINE. Neither is Dr Gardner an ordinary doctor. His researches into toxicology——

MRS PROUT. His researches are nothing to me. I wish he wasn't a doctor at all.

CHRISTINE. Even doctors have their place in the world, Mrs Prout.

MRS PROUT. They should not meddle with fiction, poking their noses——

CHRISTINE. But if fiction meddles with *them* . . . ? You know fiction is really very meddlesome. It pokes its nose with great industry.

MRS PROUT [*pulling herself together*]. Christine, you have never understood me. Let us continue.

CHRISTINE [*with an offended air, turning once more to her notebook*]. " ' Damn ! ' said the doctor, ' so I have.' "

MRS PROUT [*coughing*]. New line. "A smile flashed across the lips of Isabel as she took up a glittering knife——" [*Gives a great sob.*] Oh, Christine! I'm sure Dr Gardner wrote it.

CHRISTINE. Very well, madam. He wrote it. We have at last settled something. [MRS PROUT *buries her face in her hands.* CHRISTINE *looks up, and after an instant's pause springs towards her.*] You poor dear! You are perfectly hysterical this morning. You must go and lie down for a little. A horizontal posture is what you need.

MRS PROUT. Perhaps you are right. I will leave you for an hour. [*Totters to her feet.*] Take down this note for Dr Gardner. He may call this morning. In fact, I rather think he will. " The answer to the question is ' No ' "—capital N.

CHRISTINE. Shall I sign it ?

MRS PROUT. Yes ; sign it " C. P." And if he comes, give it him yourself, and say that I can see no one. And, Christine, would you mind [*crying gently again*] seeing the b-b-butler, and try to reason him into a sensible attitude towards my n-n-novels ? In my present state of health I couldn't stand any change. And he is so admirable at table.

CHRISTINE. Shall I offer some compromise in our next novel ? I might inquire what is the irreducible minimum of his demands.

MRS PROUT [*faintly*]. Anything, anything, if he will stay.

CHRISTINE [*following* MRS PROUT *to the door, and touching her shoulder caressingly*]. Try to sleep.

[*Exit* MRS PROUT. CHRISTINE *whistles in a low tone as she returns meditatively to her seat.*

CHRISTINE [*looking at her notebook*]. " Isabel took up a glittering knife," did she ? " The answer to the question is ' No,' " with a capital N. " C. P." sounds like Carter Paterson. Now, as I have nothing to do, I think I will devote the morning to an article on " Hysteria in Lady Novelists." Um ! Ah ! " The answer to the question is ' No ' "—capital N. What question ? Can it be that the lily-white hand of the author of *Heart Ache* has . . . ? [*Knock.*] Come in.

Enter DR GARDNER

GARDNER. Oh, good morning, Miss Feversham.

CHRISTINE. Good morning, Dr Gardner. You seem surprised to see me here. Yet I am to be found in this chair daily at this hour.

GARDNER. Not at all, not at all. I assure you I fully

expected to find both you and the chair. I also expected to find Mrs Prout.

CHRISTINE. Are you capable of interrupting our literary labours ? We do not receive callers so early, Dr Gardner. Which reminds me that I have several times remarked that this study ought not to have a door opening into the corridor.

GARDNER. As for that, may I venture to offer the excuse that I had an appointment with Mrs Prout ?

CHRISTINE. At what hour ? She never makes appointments before noon.

GARDNER. I believe she did say twelve o'clock.

CHRISTINE [*looking at her watch*]. And it is now twenty-five minutes to ten. Punctuality is a virtue. You may be said to have raised it to the dignity of a fine art.

GARDNER. I will wait. [*Sits down.*] I trust that I do not interrupt ?

CHRISTINE. Yes, Doctor, I regret to say that you do. I was about to commence the composition of an article.

GARDNER. Upon what ?

CHRISTINE. Upon " Hysteria in Lady Novelists." It is my speciality.

GARDNER. Surely lady novelists are not hysterical ?

CHRISTINE. The increase of hysteria among that class of persons is one of the saddest features of the age.

GARDNER. Dear me ! [*Enthusiastically*] But I can tell you the name of one lady novelist who isn't hysterical—and that, perhaps, the greatest name of all—Mrs Prout.

CHRISTINE. *Of course* not, of course not, Doctor. Nevertheless, Mrs Prout is somewhat indisposed this morning.

GARDNER. Cora—ill ! What is it ? Nothing serious ?

CHRISTINE. Rest assured. The merest slight indisposition. Just sufficient to delay us an hour or two with our work. Nothing more. Nerves, you know. The imagination of a great artist, Dr Gardner, is often too active, too stressful, for the frail physical organism.

GARDNER. Ah! You regard Mrs Prout as a great artist?

CHRISTINE. Doctor—even to ask such a question . . .! Do not you?

GARDNER. I? To me she is unique. I say, Miss Feversham, were you ever in love?

CHRISTINE. In love? I have had preferences.

GARDNER. Among men?

CHRISTINE. No; among boys. Recollect I am only twenty, though singularly precocious in shrewdness and calm judgment.

GARDNER. Twenty? You amaze me, Miss Feversham. I have often been struck by your common sense and knowledge of the world. They would do credit to a woman of fifty.

CHRISTINE. I am glad to notice that you do not stoop to offer me vulgar compliments about my face.

GARDNER. I am incapable of such conduct. I esteem your mental qualities too highly. And so you have had your preferences among boys?

CHRISTINE. Yes, I like to catch them from eighteen to twenty. They are so sweet and fresh then, like new milk. The *employé* of the Express Dairy Company who leaves me my half-pint at my lodgings each morning is a perfectly lovely dear. I adore him.

GARDNER. He is one of your preferences, then?

CHRISTINE. A preference among milkmen, of whom, as I change my lodgings frequently, I have known many. Then there is the postman—not a day more than eighteen, I am sure, though that is contrary to the regulations of St Martin's-le-Grand. Dr Gardner, you *should* see my postman. When *he* brings them I can receive even rejected articles with equanimity.

GARDNER. I should be charmed to see him. But tell me, Miss Feversham, have you had no serious preferences?

CHRISTINE. You seem interested in this question of preferences.

GARDNER. I am.

CHRISTINE. Doctor, I will open my heart to you. It is conceivable you may be of use to me. You are on friendly terms with Adrian, and doubtless you know the history of his exit from this house. [GARDNER *nods, with a smile.*] Doctor, he and I are passionately attached to each other. Our ages are precisely alike. It is a beautiful idyll, or rather it would be, if dear Mrs Prout did not try to transform it into a tragedy. She has not only turned the darling boy out, but she has absolutely forbidden him the house.

GARDNER. Doubtless she had her reasons.

CHRISTINE. Oh, I'm *sure* she had. Only, you see, her reasons aren't ours. Of course we could marry at once if we chose. I could easily keep Adrian. I do not, however, wish to inconvenience dear Mrs Prout. It is a mistake to quarrel with the rich relations of one's future husband. But I was thinking that perhaps you, Doctor, might persuade dear Mrs Prout that my marriage to Adrian need not necessarily interfere with the performance of my duties as her secretary.

GARDNER. Anything that I can do, Miss Feversham, you may rely on me doing.

CHRISTINE. You are a dear.

GARDNER. But why should you imagine that I have any influence with Mrs Prout?

CHRISTINE. I do not imagine; I know. It is my unerring insight over again, my faultless observation. Doctor, you did not begin to question me about love because you were interested in *my* love affairs, but because you were interested in your own, and couldn't keep off the subject. I read you like a book. You love Mrs Prout, my dear Doctor. Therefore you have influence over her. No woman is uninfluenced by the man who loves her.

GARDNER [*laughing between self-satisfaction and self-consciousness*]. You have noticed that I admire Mrs Prout ? It appears that nothing escapes you.

CHRISTINE. That is a trifle. The butler has noticed it.

GARDNER. The butler !

CHRISTINE. The butler.

GARDNER [*with abandon*]. Let him. Let the whole world notice. Miss Feversham, be it known that I love Mrs Prout with passionate adoration. Before the day is out I shall either be her affianced bridegroom—or I shall be a dead man.

CHRISTINE [*leaning forward, in a low, tense voice*]. You proposed to her last night ?

GARDNER. I did.

CHRISTINE. And you were to come for the answer this morning ?

GARDNER. Yes. Can you not guess that I am eager—excited ? Can you not pardon me for thinking it is noon at twenty-five minutes to ten ? Ah, Miss Feversham, if Adrian adores you with one-tenth of the fire with which I adore Mrs Prout——

CHRISTINE. Stop, Doctor, I do not wish to be a burnt sacrifice. Now let me ask you a question. You have seen that attack on Mrs Prout, entitled " Medicine in Fiction," in this month's *Forum*. Do you know the author of it ?

GARDNER. I don't. Has it disturbed Mrs Prout ?

CHRISTINE. It has. Did she not mention it to you ?

GARDNER. Not a word. If I did know the author of it, if I ever do know the author of it, I will tear him [*fiercely*] limb from limb.

THE STEPMOTHER

CHRISTINE. I trust you will chloroform him first. It will be horrid of you if you don't.

GARDNER. I absolutely decline to chloroform him first.

CHRISTINE. You must.

GARDNER. I won't.

CHRISTINE. Never mind. Perhaps you will be dead. Remember that you have promised to kill yourself to-day on a certain contingency. Should you really do it? Should you really put an end to your life if Mrs Prout gave you a refusal?

GARDNER. I swear it. Existence would be valueless to me.

CHRISTINE. By the way, Mrs Prout told me that if you called I was to say that she could see no one.

GARDNER. See no one! But she promised . . .

CHRISTINE. However, she left a note.

GARDNER [*starting up*]. Give it to me instantly. Why didn't you give it me before?

CHRISTINE. I had no opportunity. Besides, I haven't transcribed it yet. It was dictated.

GARDNER. *Dictated?* Are you sure?

CHRISTINE [*seriously*]. Oh, yes, she dictates *everything*.

GARDNER. Well, well, read it to me. Quick, I say.

CHRISTINE [*turning over leaves rapidly*]. Here it is. Are you listening?

GARDNER. Great Heaven!

CHRISTINE [*reads from her shorthand notes*]. "The answer to your question is——"

GARDNER. Go on.

CHRISTINE [*drawing her breath first*]. "Yes.—C. P." There! I've saved your life for you.

GARDNER. You have indeed, my dear girl. But I must see her. I must see my beloved Cora.

CHRISTINE [*taking his hand*]. Accept my advice, Doctor—

the advice of a simple, artless girl. Do not attempt to see her to-day. There are seasons of emotion when a woman [*Stops.*] . . . Go downstairs and write to her, and then give the letter to me. [*Pats him on the back.*]

GARDNER. I will, by Jove. Miss Feversham, you're a good sort. And as you've told me something, I'll tell you something. Adrian is going to storm the castle to-day.

CHRISTINE. Adrian! [*A knock.*

Enter ADRIAN

ADRIAN. Since you command it, I enter.

GARDNER. Let me pass, bold youth.

[*Exit* DR GARDNER *hurriedly*.

ADRIAN [*overcome by* GARDNER's *haste*]. Why this avalanche? Has something happened suddenly?

CHRISTINE. Several things have happened suddenly, Adrian, and several more will probably happen when your mamma discovers that you are defying her orders in this audacious manner. Why are you here? [*Kisses him.*] You perfect duck!

ADRIAN [*gravely*]. I am not here, Miss Feversham——

CHRISTINE. "Miss Feversham"—and my kiss still warm on his lips!

ADRIAN. I repeat, Miss Feversham, that I am not here. This [*pointing to himself*] is not I. It is merely a rather smart member of the staff of the *Daily Snail*, come to interview Cora Prout, the celebrated novelist.

CHRISTINE. And I have kissed a *Snail* reporter. Ugh!

ADRIAN. Impetuosity has ruined many women.

CHRISTINE. It is a morning of calamities. [*Assuming the secretarial pose*] Your card, please.

ADRIAN [*handing card*]. With pleasure.

CHRISTINE [*taking card by the extreme corner, perusing it*

with disdain, and then dropping it on the floor]. We never see interviewers in the morning.

ADRIAN. Then I will call this afternoon.

CHRISTINE. You must write for an appointment.

ADRIAN. Oh! I'll take my chances, thanks.

CHRISTINE. We never give them: it is our rule. We have to be very particular. The fact is, we hate being interviewed, and we only submit to the process out of a respectful regard for the great and enlightened public. Any sort of notoriety, any suggestion of self-advertisement, is distasteful to us. What do you wish to interview us about? If it's the new novel, we are absolutely mum. Accept that from me.

ADRIAN. It isn't the new novel. The *Snail* wishes to know whether Mrs Prout feels inclined to make any statement in reply to that article, "Medicine in Fiction," in the *Forum*.

CHRISTINE. Oh, Adrian, do you know anything about that article?

ADRIAN. Rather! I know *all* about it.

CHRISTINE. You treasure! You invaluable darling! I will marry you to-morrow morning by special license——

ADRIAN. Recollect, it is a *Snail* reporter whom you are addressing. Suppose I were to print that!

CHRISTINE. Just so. You are prudence itself, while I, for the moment, happen to be a little—a little abnormal. I saved a man's life this morning, and it is apt to upset one's nerves. It is a dreadful thing to do—to save a man's life. And the consequences will be simply frightful for me. [*Buries her face in her hands.*]

ADRIAN. Christine [*taking her hands*], what are you raving about? You are not yourself.

CHRISTINE. I wish I wasn't. [*Looking up with forced calm*] Adrian, there is a possibility of your being able to save me from the results of my horrible act, if only you will tell me the name of the author of that article in the *Forum*.

ADRIAN [*tenderly*]. Christine, you little know what you ask. But for you I will do anything. . . . Kiss me, my white lily. [*She kisses him.*]

CHRISTINE [*whispers*]. Tell me.

[*He folds her in his arms.*

Enter MRS PROUT, *excitedly*

MRS PROUT [*as she enters*]. Christine, that appalling butler has actually left the house. . . . [*Observing group*] Heavens!

CHRISTINE [*quietly disengaging herself*]. You seem a little better, Mrs Prout. A person to interview you from the *Daily Snail* [*pointing to* ADRIAN].

MRS PROUT. Adrian!

ADRIAN. Yes, Mamma.

MRS PROUT [*opening her lips to speak and then closing them*]. Sit down.

ADRIAN. Certainly, Mamma. [*Sits.*]

MRS PROUT. How dare you come here?

ADRIAN. I don't know how, Mamma. [*Picks up his card from the floor and hands it to her; then resumes his seat.*]

MRS PROUT [*glancing at card*]. Pah!

CHRISTINE. That's just what I told the person, Mrs Prout. [MRS PROUT *burns her up with a glance.*]

MRS PROUT. You have, then, abandoned your medical studies, for which I had paid all the fees?

ADRIAN. Yes, Mamma. You see, I was obliged to earn something at once. So I took to journalism. I am getting on quite nicely. The editor of the *Snail* says that I may review your next book.

MRS PROUT. Unnatural stepson, to review in cold blood

the novel of your own stepmother! But this morning I am getting used to misfortunes.

ADRIAN. It cuts me to the heart to hear you refer to any action of mine as a misfortune for you. Perhaps you would prefer that I should at once relieve you of my presence?

MRS PROUT. Decidedly, yes—that is, if Christine thinks she can do without the fifth act of that caress which I interrupted.

CHRISTINE. The curtain was already falling, madam.

MRS PROUT. Very well. [*To Adrian*] Good-day.

ADRIAN. As a stepson I retire. As the " special " of the *Daily Snail* I must insist on remaining. A " special " of the *Daily Snail* is incapable of being snubbed. He knows what he wants, and he gets it, or he ceases to be a " special " of the *Daily Snail*.

MRS PROUT. I esteem the Press, and though I should prefer an existence of absolute privacy, I never refuse its demands. I sacrifice myself to my public, freely acknowledging that a great artist has no exclusive right to the details of his own daily life. A great artist belongs to the world. What is it you want, Mr Snail?

ADRIAN. I want to know whether you care to say anything in reply to that article on " Medicine in Fiction " in the *Forum*.

MRS PROUT [*sinking back in despair*]. That article again! [*Sitting up*] Tell me—do you know the author?

ADRIAN. I do.

MRS PROUT. His name!

ADRIAN. He is a friend of mine.

MRS PROUT. His name!

ADRIAN. I am informed that in writing it he was actuated by the highest motives. His desire was not only to make a little money, but to revenge himself against a person who had deeply injured him. He didn't know much about medicine, being only a student, and probably the larger part of his arguments could not be sustained, but he knew enough to make a show, and he made it.

MRS PROUT. His name! I insist.

ADRIAN. Adrian Spout or Prout — I have a poor memory. . . .

MRS PROUT. Is it possible?

CHRISTINE. Monster!

ADRIAN. Need I defend myself, Mamma? Consider what you had done to me. You had devastated my young heart, which was just unfolding to its first passion. You had blighted the springtime of the exquisite creature [*looking at* CHRISTINE, *who is moved by the feeling in his tones*] —the exquisite creature who was dearer to me than all the world. In place of the luxury of my late father's house you offered me—the street. . . .

CHRISTINE. Yes . . . and Gower Street.

ADRIAN. You, who should have gently fostered and encouraged the frail buds of my energy and intelligence— you cast me forth . . .

CHRISTINE. Cast *them* forth.

ADRIAN. Cast *them* forth, untimely plucked, to wither, and perhaps die, in the deserts of a great city. And for what? For what?

CHRISTINE. Merely lest she should be deprived of *my* poor services. Ah! Mrs Prout, can you wonder that Mr Adrian should actively resent such conduct—you with your marvellous knowledge of human nature?

MRS PROUT. Adrian, did you really write it?

ADRIAN. Why, of course. You seem rather pleased than otherwise, Mamma.

MRS PROUT [*after cogitating*]. Ah! You didn't write it, really. You are just boasting. It is a plot, a plot!

THE STEPMOTHER

ADRIAN. I can prove that I wrote it, since you impugn my veracity.

MRS PROUT. How can you prove it?

ADRIAN. By producing the cheque which I received from the *Forum* this very morning.

MRS PROUT. Produce it, and I will forgive all.

ADRIAN [*with a sign to* CHRISTINE *that he entirely fails to comprehend the situation*]. I fly. It is in my humble attic, round the corner. Back in two minutes.   [*Exit* ADRIAN.

MRS PROUT. Christine, *did* he really write it?

CHRISTINE. Can you doubt his word? Was it for lying that you ejected the poor youth from this residence?

MRS PROUT. Ah! If he did! [*Smiles.*] Of course Dr Gardner has not called?

CHRISTINE. Yes, he was in about twenty minutes ago.

MRS PROUT [*agonised*]. Did you give him my note?

CHRISTINE. No.

MRS PROUT. Thank heaven!

CHRISTINE. I had not copied it out, so I read it to him.

MRS PROUT. You read it to him?

CHRISTINE. Yes; that seemed the obvious thing to do.

MRS PROUT [*in black despair*]. All is over.   [*Sinks back.*

Enter DR GARDNER *hastily*

GARDNER [*excited*]. I was looking out of the window of my flat when I saw Adrian tear along the street. I said to myself, "A man, even a reporter, only runs like that when a doctor is required, and urgently required. Some one is ill, perhaps my darling Cora." So I flew upstairs.

MRS PROUT [*with a shriek*]. Dr Gardner!

GARDNER. You *are* indeed ill, my beloved. [*Approaching her*] What is the matter?

MRS PROUT [*waving him off*]. It is nothing, Doctor. Could you get me some salts? I have mislaid mine. [*Sighs.*]

GARDNER. Salts! In an instant. [*Exit* DR GARDNER.

MRS PROUT. Christine, you said you read my note to Dr Gardner.

CHRISTINE. Yes, Mrs Prout.

MRS PROUT. His behaviour is singular in the extreme. He seems positively overjoyed, while the freedom of his endearing epithets—— What were the precise terms I used? Read me the note.

CHRISTINE. Yes, Mrs Prout. [*Reads demurely*] "The answer to your question is 'Yes'"—with a capital N.

MRS PROUT. "Yes" with a capital N?

CHRISTINE [*calmly*]. I mean with a capital Y.

[CHRISTINE *and* MRS PROUT *look steadily at each other. Then they both smile.*

Enter DR GARDNER

GARDNER [*handing the salts*]. You are sure you are not ill?

MRS PROUT [*smiling at him radiantly*]. I am convinced of it. Christine, will you kindly reach me down the dictionary from that shelf?

[*While* CHRISTINE'S *back is turned* DR GARDNER *gives, and* MRS PROUT *returns, a passionate kiss.*

CHRISTINE [*handing dictionary*]. Here it is, Mrs Prout.

MRS PROUT [*after consulting it*]. I thought I could not be mistaken. Christine, you have rendered me a service [*regarding her affectionately*]—a service for which I shall not forget to express my gratitude; but I am obliged to dismiss you instantly from my service.

CHRISTINE. Dismiss me, madam?

GARDNER. Cora, can you be so cruel?

MRS PROUT. Alas, yes! She has sinned the secretarial sin which is beyond forgiveness. She has misspelt.

GARDNER. Impossible!

MRS PROUT. It is too true.

THE STEPMOTHER

GARDNER. Tell me the sad details.

MRS PROUT. She has been guilty of spelling " No " with a " Y."

GARDNER. Dear me! And a word of one syllable, too! Miss Feversham, I should not have thought it of you.

Enter ADRIAN

ADRIAN [*as he hands a cheque for* MRS PROUT'S *inspection*]. Here again, Doctor?

GARDNER. Yes, and to stay.

MRS PROUT. Adrian, the Doctor and I are engaged to be married. And talking of marriage, you observe that girl there in the corner? Take her and marry her at the earliest convenient moment. She is no longer my secretary.

ADRIAN. What! You consent?

MRS PROUT. I consent.

ADRIAN. And you pardon my article?

MRS PROUT. No, my dear Adrian, I ignore it. Here, take your ill-gotten gains. [*Returning cheque*] They will bring you no good. And since they will bring you no good, I have decided to allow you the sum of five hundred pounds a year. You must have something.

ADRIAN. Stepmother!

CHRISTINE [*advancing to take* MRS PROUT'S *hand*]. Stepmother-in-law!

GARDNER. Cora, you are an angel.

MRS PROUT. Merely an artist, my dear Tom, merely an artist. I have the dramatic sense—that is all.

ADRIAN. Your sense is more than dramatic, it is common; it is even horse. What about the *Snail* " special," Mummy?

MRS PROUT. My attitude is one of strict silence.

ADRIAN. But I must go away with something.

MRS PROUT. Strict silence. The attack is beneath my notice.

ADRIAN. But what can I *say*?

CHRISTINE. Say that Mrs Prout's late secretary, Miss Feversham, having retired from her post, has already entered upon a career of original literary composition. That will be a nice newsy item, won't it?

ADRIAN [*taking out notebook*]. Rather! What is she at work on?

CHRISTINE. Oh, well, I scarcely——

GARDNER. I know—" Hysteria in Lady Novelists."

MRS PROUT. What?

GARDNER [*to* CHRISTINE]. Didn't you tell me so?

CHRISTINE. Of course I didn't, Doctor. What a shocking memory you have! It is worse than my spelling.

GARDNER. Then what did you say?

CHRISTINE. I said, " Generosity in Lady Novelists."

CURTAIN

Applications regarding amateur performances of this play should be addressed to Messrs James B. Pinker and Son, Talbot House, Arundel Street, Strand, London, W.C.2, or to Mr Le Roy Phillips, 41 Winter Street, Boston, Massachusetts, U.S.A.

THE MAKER OF DREAMS
A FANTASY IN ONE ACT
By Oliphant Down

OLIPHANT DOWN was one of the many promising young men who were killed in the War. He was born in 1885, and died in 1917, after winning the Military Cross. His cousin describes him in these words: "His was a most lovable nature that abhorred war and its attendant horrors. He loved everything that was beautiful in life. The realm of fantasy and charm was his delight, and the keynote of his writings. . . . It is remarkable that such a man should have become such a brilliant and gallant soldier."

"The Maker of Dreams" is a delightful Pierrot play, and illustrates the author's gift for fantasy. It was written when he was twenty-six, and was an immediate success in every country where the English language is spoken. Two years later there followed "The Dream Child," which is in a similar vein.

CHARACTERS

PIERROT
PIERRETTE
THE MANUFACTURER

This play was first produced by the Scottish Repertory Theatre Company, under the direction of Mr Alfred Wareing, at the Royalty Theatre, Glasgow, on Monday, November 20, 1911, with the following cast:

Pierrot . . . . . ELIOT MAKEHAM
Pierrette . . . . . MURIEL GIBB
The Manufacturer . . BEN FIELD

THE MAKER OF DREAMS

Evening. A room in an old cottage, with walls of dark oak, lit only by the moonlight that peers through the long, low casement-window at the back, and the glow from the fire that is burning merrily on the spectator's left. A cobbled street can be seen outside, and a door to the right of the window opens directly on to it. Opposite the fire is a kitchen dresser with cups and plates twinkling in the firelight. A high-backed oak settle, as though afraid of the cold moonlight, has turned its back on the window and warms its old timbers at the fire. In the middle of the room stands a table with a red cover; there are chairs on either side of it. On the hob, a kettle is keeping itself warm; whilst overhead, on the hood of the chimneypiece, a small lamp is turned very low.

A figure flits past the window and, with a click of the latch, PIERRETTE *enters. She hangs up her cloak by the door, gives a little shiver and runs to warm herself for a moment. Then, having turned up the lamp, she places the kettle on the fire. Crossing the room, she takes a tablecloth from the dresser and proceeds to lay tea, setting out crockery for two. Once she goes to the window and, drawing aside the common red casement curtains, looks out, but returns to her work, disappointed. She puts a spoonful of tea into the teapot, and another, and a third. Something outside attracts her attention; she listens, her face brightening. A voice is heard singing:*

" Baby, don't wait for the moon,
    She is caught in a tangle of boughs;

And mellow and musical June
　　Is saying 'Good-night' to the cows."

[*The voice draws nearer and a conical white hat goes past the window.* PIERROT *enters.*

PIERROT [*throwing his hat to* PIERRETTE]. Ugh! How cold it is. My feet are like ice.

PIERRETTE. Here are your slippers. I put them down to warm.

[*She kneels beside him, as he sits before the fire and commences to slip off his shoes.*

PIERROT [*singing*].

" Baby, don't wait for the moon,
　　She will put out her tongue and grimace;
And mellow and musical June
　　Is pinning the stars in their place."

Isn't tea ready yet?

PIERRETTE. Nearly. Only waiting for the kettle to boil.

PIERROT. How cold it was in the market-place to-day! I don't believe I sang at all well. I can't sing in the cold.

PIERRETTE. Ah, you're like the kettle. He can't sing when he's cold either. Hurry up, Mr Kettle, if you please.

PIERROT. I wish it were in love with the sound of its own voice.

PIERRETTE. I believe it is. Now it's singing like a bird. We'll make the tea with the nightingale's tongue. [*She pours the boiling water into the teapot.*] Come along.

PIERROT [*looking into the fire*]. I wonder. She had beauty, she had form, but had she soul?

PIERRETTE [*cutting bread and butter at the table*]. Come and be cheerful, instead of grumbling there to the fire.

PIERROT. I was thinking.

THE MAKER OF DREAMS

PIERRETTE. Come and have tea. When you sit by the fire, thoughts only fly up the chimney.

PIERROT. The whole world's a chimneypiece. Give people a thing as worthless as paper, and it catches fire in them and makes a stir; but real thought, they let it go up with the smoke.

PIERRETTE. Cheer up, Pierrot. See how thick I've spread the butter.

PIERROT. You're always cheerful.

PIERRETTE. I try to be happy.

PIERROT. Ugh!

> [*He has moved to the table. There is a short silence, during which* PIERROT *sips his tea moodily.*

PIERRETTE. Tea all right?

PIERROT. Middling.

PIERRETTE. Only middling! I'll pour you out some fresh.

PIERROT. Oh, it's all right! How you do worry a fellow!

PIERRETTE. Heigh-ho! Shall I chain up that big black dog?

PIERROT. I say, did you see that girl to-day?

PIERRETTE. Whereabouts?

PIERROT. Standing by the horse-trough. With a fine air, and a string of great beads.

PIERRETTE. I didn't see her.

PIERROT. I did, though. And she saw me. Watched me all the time I was singing, and clapped her hands like anything each time. I wonder if it is possible for a woman to have a soul as well as such beautiful colouring.

PIERRETTE. She was made up!

PIERROT. I'm sure she was not! And how do you know? You didn't see her.

PIERRETTE. Perhaps I *did* see her.

PIERROT. Now, look here, Pierrette, it's no good your being jealous. When you and I took on this show business, we arranged to be just partners and nothing more. If I see any one I want to marry, I shall marry 'em. And if you see any one who wants to marry you, *you* can marry 'em.

PIERRETTE. I'm not jealous! It's absurd!

PIERROT [*singing abstractedly*].

"Baby, don't wait for the moon,
    She has scratched her white chin on the gorse;
And mellow and musical June
    Is bringing the cuckoo remorse."

PIERRETTE. Did you see that girl after the show?

PIERROT. No. She had slipped away in the crowd. Here, I've had enough tea. I shall go out and try to find her.

PIERRETTE. Why don't you stay in by the fire? You could help me to darn the socks.

PIERROT. Don't try to chaff me. Darning, indeed! I hope life has got something better in it than darning.

PIERRETTE. I doubt it. It's pretty much the same all the world over. First we wear holes in our socks, and then we mend them. The wise ones are those who make the best of it, and darn as well as they can.

PIERROT. I say, that gives me an idea for a song.

PIERRETTE. Out with it, then.

PIERROT. Well, I haven't exactly formed it yet. This is what flashed through my mind as you spoke:

    [*He runs up on to the table, using it as a stage.*

"Life's a ball of worsted,
    Unwind it if you can,
You who oft have boasted

    [*He pauses for a moment, then hurriedly, in order to gloss over the false accenting.*

That you are a man."

Of course that's only a rough idea.

THE MAKER OF DREAMS

PIERRETTE. Are you going to sing it at the show?

PIERROT [*jumping down from the table*]. You're always so lukewarm. A man of artistic ideas is as sensitively skinned as a baby.

PIERRETTE. Do stay in, Pierrot. It's so cold outside.

PIERROT. You want me to listen to you grumbling, I suppose.

PIERRETTE. Just now you said I was always cheerful.

PIERROT. There you are; girding at me again.

PIERRETTE. I'm sorry, Pierrot. But the market-place is dreadfully wet, and your shoes are awfully thin.

PIERROT. I tell you I will not stop in. I'm going out to find that girl. How do I know she isn't the very woman of my dreams?

PIERRETTE. Why are you always trying to picture an ideal woman?

PIERROT. Don't *you ever* picture an ideal man?

PIERRETTE. No, I try to be practical.

PIERROT. Women are so unimaginative! They are such pathetic, motherly things, and when they feel extra motherly, they say, " I'm in love." All that is so sordid and petty. I want a woman I can set on a pedestal, and just look up at her and love her.

PIERRETTE [*speaking very fervently*].

" Pierrot, don't wait for the moon,
    There's a heart chilling cold in her rays;
  And mellow and musical June
    Will only last thirty short days."

PIERROT. Oh, I should never make you understand! Well, I'm off.

[*As he goes out, he sings, sidelong, over his shoulder in a mocking tone,* " Baby, don't wait for the moon."
PIERRETTE *listens for a moment to his voice dying*

away in the distance. Then she moves to the fireplace, and begins to stir the fire. As she kneels there, the words of an old recitation form on her lips. Half unconsciously she recites it again to an audience of laughing flames and glowing, thoughtful coals.

" There lives a maid in the big, wide world,
   By the crowded town and mart,
And people sigh as they pass her by ;
   They call her Hungry Heart.

" For there trembles that on her red rose lip
   That never her tongue can say,
And her eyes are sad, and she is not glad
   In the beautiful calm of day.

" Deep down in the waters of pure, clear thought,
   The mate of her fancy lies ;
Sleeping, the night is made fair by his light
   Sweet kiss on her dreaming eyes.

" Though a man was made in the wells of time
   Who could set her soul on fire,
Her life unwinds, and she never finds
   This love of her heart's desire.

" If you meet this maid of a hopeless love,
   Play not a meddler's part.
Silence were best ; let her keep in her breast
   The dream of her hungry heart."

   [*Overcome by tears, she hides her face in her hands. A slow, treble knock comes on the door ;* PIERRETTE *looks up wonderingly. Again the knock sounds.*

PIERRETTE. Come in.

   [*The door swings slowly open, as though of its own accord, and without, on the threshold, is seen the* MANUFACTURER, *standing full in the moonlight.*

THE MAKER OF DREAMS

He is a curious, though kindly looking, old man, and yet, with all his years, he does not appear to be the least infirm. He is the sort of person that children take to instinctively. He wears a quaintly cut, bottle-green coat, with silver buttons and large side-pockets, which almost hide his knee-breeches. His shoes have large buckles and red heels. He is exceedingly unlike a prosperous manufacturer, and, but for the absence of a violin, would be mistaken for a village fiddler. Without a word he advances into the room, and, again of its own accord, the door closes noiselessly behind him.

PIERRETTE [*jumping up and moving towards him*]. Oh, I'm so sorry. I ought to have opened the door when you knocked.

MANUFACTURER. That's all right. I'm used to opening doors. And yours opens much more easily than some I come across. Would you believe it, some people positively nail their doors up, and it's no good knocking. But there you're wondering who I am.

PIERRETTE. I was wondering if you were hungry.

MANUFACTURER. Ah, a woman's instinct. But, thank you, no. I am a small eater; I might say a very small eater. A smile or a squeeze of the hand keeps me going admirably.

PIERRETTE. At least you'll sit down and make yourself at home.

MANUFACTURER [*moving to the settle*]. Well, I have a habit of making myself at home everywhere. In fact, most people think you can't make a *home* without *me*. May I put my feet on the fender? It's an old habit of mine. I always do it.

PIERRETTE. They say round here:

"Without feet on the fender
Love is but slender."

MANUFACTURER. Quite right. It is the whole secret of the domestic fireside. Pierrette, you have been crying.

PIERRETTE. I believe I have.

MANUFACTURER. Bless you, I know all about it. It's Pierrot. And so you're in love with him, and he doesn't care a little bit about you, eh? What a strange old world it is! And you cry your eyes out over him.

PIERRETTE. Oh, no, I don't often cry. But to-night he seemed more grumpy than usual, and I tried so hard to cheer him up.

MANUFACTURER. Grumpy, is he?

PIERRETTE. He doesn't mean it, though. It's the cold weather, and the show hasn't been paying so well lately. Pierrot wants to write an article about us for the local paper by way of an advertisement. He thinks the editor may print it if he gives him free passes for his family.

MANUFACTURER. Do you think Pierrot is worth your tears?

PIERRETTE. Oh, yes!

MANUFACTURER. You know, tears are not to be wasted. We only have a certain amount of them given to us just for keeping the heart moist. And when we've used them all up and haven't any more, the heart dries up, too.

PIERRETTE. Pierrot is a splendid fellow. You don't know him as well as I do. It's true he's always discontented, but it's only because he's not in love with any one. You know, love does make a tremendous difference in a man.

MANUFACTURER. That's true enough. And has it made a difference in you?

PIERRETTE. Oh, yes! I put Pierrot's slippers down to warm, and I make tea for him, and all the time I'm happy because I'm doing something for him. If I weren't in love, I should find it a drudgery.

MANUFACTURER. Are you sure it's real love?

PIERRETTE. Why, yes!

THE MAKER OF DREAMS

MANUFACTURER. Every time you think of Pierrot, do you hear the patter of little bare feet ? And every time he speaks, do you feel little chubby hands on your breast and face ?

PIERRETTE [*fervently*]. Yes ! Oh, yes ! That's just it !

MANUFACTURER. You've got it right enough. But why is it that Pierrot can wake up all this poetry in you ?

PIERRETTE. Because—oh, because he's just Pierrot.

MANUFACTURER. " Because he's just Pierrot." The same old reason.

PIERRETTE. Of course, he is a bit dreamy. But that's his soul. I am sure he could do great things if he tried. And have you noticed his smile ? Isn't it lovely ! Sometimes, when he's not looking, I want ever so much to try it on, just to see how I should look in it. [*Pensively*] But I wish he'd smile at me a little more often, instead of at others.

MANUFACTURER. Ho ! So he smiles at others, does he ?

PIERRETTE. Hardly a day goes by but there's some fine lady at the show. There was one there to-day, a tall girl with red cheeks. He is gone to look for her now. And it is not their faults. The poor things can't help being in love with him. [*Proudly*] I believe every one is in love with Pierrot.

MANUFACTURER. But supposing one of these fine ladies were to marry him ?

PIERRETTE. Oh, they'd never do that. A fine lady would never marry a poor singer. If Pierrot were to get married, I think I should just . . . fade away. . . . Oh, but I don't know why I talk to you like this. I feel as if I had known you for a long, long time.

> [*The* MANUFACTURER *rises from the settle and moves across to* PIERRETTE, *who is now folding up the white tablecloth.*

MANUFACTURER [*very slowly*]. Perhaps you *have* known me for a long, long time.

> [*His tone is so kindly and impressive that* PIERRETTE *forgets the tablecloth and looks up at him. For a moment or two he smiles back at her as she gazes, spellbound; then he turns away to the fire again, with the little chuckle that is never far from his lips.*

PIERRETTE [*taking a small bow from his side-pocket*]. Oh, look at this.

MANUFACTURER [*in mock alarm*]. Oh, oh, I didn't mean you to see that. I'd forgotten it was sticking out of my pocket. I used to do a lot of archery at one time. I don't get much chance now. [*He takes it and puts it back in his pocket.*]

PIERROT [*singing in the distance*].

> " Baby, don't wait for the moon,
>   She is drawing the sea in her net;
> And mellow and musical June
>   Is teaching the rose to forget."

MANUFACTURER [*in a whisper as the voice draws nearer*]. Who is that?

PIERRETTE. Pierrot.

> [*Again the conical white hat flashes past the window, and* PIERROT *enters.*

PIERROT. I can't find her anywhere. [*Seeing the* MANUFACTURER] Hullo! Who are you?

MANUFACTURER. I am a stranger to you, but Pierrette knew me in a moment.

PIERROT. An old flame perhaps?

MANUFACTURER. True, I am an old flame. I've lighted up the world for a considerable time. Yet when you say "old," there are many people who think I'm wonderfully well preserved for my age. How long do you think I've been trotting about?

THE MAKER OF DREAMS

PIERROT [*testily, measuring a length with his hands*]. Oh, about that long.

MANUFACTURER. I suppose being funny all day *does* get on your nerves.

PIERRETTE. Pierrot, you needn't be rude.

MANUFACTURER [*anxious to be alone with* PIERROT]. Pierrette, have you got supper in?

PIERRETTE. Oh, I must fly! The shops will all be shut. Will you be here when I come back?

MANUFACTURER [*bustling her out*]. I can't promise, but I'll try, I'll try.

> [PIERRETTE *goes out. There is a silence, during which the* MANUFACTURER *regards* PIERROT *with amusement.*

MANUFACTURER. Well, friend Pierrot, so business is not very brisk.

PIERROT. Brisk! If laughter meant business, it would be brisk enough, but there's no money. However, I've done one good piece of work to-day. I've arranged with the editor to put an article in the paper. That will fetch 'em. [*Singing*]

> " Please come one day and see our house that's down among the trees,
> But do not come at four o'clock for then we count the bees,
> And bath the tadpoles and the frogs, who splash the clouds with gold,
> And watch the new-cut cucum*bers* perspiring with the cold."

That's a song I'm writing.

MANUFACTURER. Pierrot, if you had all the money in the world you wouldn't be happy.

PIERROT. Wouldn't I? Give me all the money in the

world and I'll risk it. To start with, I'd build schools to educate the people up to high-class things.

MANUFACTURER. You dream of fame and wealth and empty ideals, and you miss all the best things there are. You are discontented. Why? Because you don't know how to be happy.

PIERROT [*reciting*].

> "Life's a running brooklet,
> Catch the fishes there,
> You who wrote a booklet
> On a woman's hair."

[*Explaining*] That's another song I'm writing. It's the second verse. Things come to me all of a sudden like that. I must run out a third verse, just to wind it up.

MANUFACTURER. Why don't you write a song without any end, one that goes on for ever?

PIERROT. I say, that's rather silly, isn't it?

MANUFACTURER. It all depends. For a song of that sort the singer must be always happy.

PIERROT. That wants a bit of doing in my line.

MANUFACTURER. Shall you and I transact a little business?

PIERROT. By all means. What seats would you like? There are the front rows covered in velvet, one shilling; wooden benches behind, sixpence; and, right at the back, the twopenny part. But, of course, you'll have shilling ones. How many shall we say?

MANUFACTURER. You don't know who I am.

PIERROT. That makes no difference. All are welcome, and we thank you for your courteous attention.

MANUFACTURER. Pierrot, I am a maker of dreams.

PIERROT. A what?

MANUFACTURER. I make all the dreams that float about this musty world.

THE MAKER OF DREAMS

PIERROT. I say, you'd better have a rest for a bit. I expect you're a trifle done up.

MANUFACTURER. Pierrot, Pierrot, your superior mind can't tumble to my calling. A child or one of the 'people' would in a moment. I am a maker of dreams, little things that glide about into people's hearts and make them glad. Haven't you often wondered where the swallows go to in the autumn ? They come to my workshop, and tell me who wants a dream, and what happened to the dreams they took with them in the spring.

PIERROT. Oh, I say, you can't expect me to believe that.

MANUFACTURER. When flowers fade, have you never wondered where their colours go to, or what becomes of all the butterflies in the winter ? There isn't much winter about my workshop.

PIERROT. I had never thought of it before.

MANUFACTURER. It's a kind of lost property office, where every beautiful thing that the world has neglected finds its way. And there I make my celebrated dream, the dream that is called 'love.'

PIERROT. Ho ! ho ! Now we're talking.

MANUFACTURER. You don't believe in it ?

PIERROT. Yes, in a way. But it doesn't last. It doesn't last. If there is form, there isn't soul, and, if there is soul, there isn't form. Oh, I've tried hard enough to believe it, but, after the first wash, the colours run.

MANUFACTURER. You only got hold of a substitute. Wait until you see the genuine article.

PIERROT. But how is one to tell it ?

MANUFACTURER. There are heaps of signs. As soon as you get the real thing, your shoulder-blades begin to tingle. That's love's wings sprouting. And, next, you want to soar up among the stars and sit on the roof of heaven and sing to the moon. Of course, that's because I put such a lot of the moon into my dreams. I break bits off until it's nearly all gone, and then I let it grow big again. It grows very quickly, as I dare say you've noticed. After a fortnight it is ready for use once more.

PIERROT. This is most awfully fascinating. And do the swallows bring all the dreams?

MANUFACTURER. Not always; I have other messengers. Every night when the big clock strikes twelve, a day slips down from the calendar, and runs away to my workshop in the Land of Long Ago. I give him a touch of scarlet and a gleam of gold, and say, "Go back, little Yesterday, and be a memory in the world." But my best dreams I keep for to-day. I buy babies, and fit them up with a dream, and then send them complete and carriage paid . . . in the usual manner.

PIERROT. I've been dreaming all my life, but they've always been dreams I made myself. I suppose I don't mix 'em properly.

MANUFACTURER. You leave out the very essence of them. You must put in a little sorrow, just to take away the over-sweetness. I found that out very soon, so I took a little of the fresh dew that made pearls in the early morning, and I sprinkled my dreams with the gift of tears.

PIERROT [*ecstatically*]. The gift of tears! How beautiful! You know, I should rather like to try a real one. Not one of my own making.

MANUFACTURER. Well, there are plenty about, if you only look for them.

PIERROT. That is all very well, but who's going to look about for stray dreams?

MANUFACTURER. I once made a dream that would just suit you. I slipped it inside a baby. That was twenty years ago, and the baby is now a full-grown woman, with great blue eyes and fair hair.

PIERROT. It's a lot of use merely telling me about her.

THE MAKER OF DREAMS

MANUFACTURER. I'll do more. When I shipped her to the world, I kept the bill of lading. Here it is. You shall have it.

PIERROT. Thanks, but what's the good of it?

MANUFACTURER. Why, the holder of that is able to claim the goods; you will notice it contains a complete description, too. I promise you, you're in luck.

PIERROT. Has she red cheeks and a string of great beads?

MANUFACTURER. No.

PIERROT. Ah, then it is not she. Where shall I find her?

MANUFACTURER. That's for you to discover. All you have to do is to search.

PIERROT. I'll start at once. [*He moves as if to go.*

MANUFACTURER. I shouldn't start out to-night.

PIERROT. But I want to find her soon. Somebody else may find her before me.

MANUFACTURER. Pierrot, there was once a man who wanted to gather mushrooms.

PIERROT [*annoyed at the commonplace*]. Mushrooms!

MANUFACTURER. Fearing people would be up before him, he started out overnight. Morning came, and he found none, so he returned disconsolate to his house. As he came through the garden, he found a great mushroom had grown up in the night by his very door-step. Take the advice of one who knows, and wait a bit.

PIERROT. If that's your advice . . . But tell me this, do you think I shall find her?

MANUFACTURER. I can't say for certain. Would you consider yourself a fool?

PIERROT. Ah . . . of course . . . when you ask me a direct thing like that, you make it . . . er . . . rather awkward for me. But, if I may say so, as man to ma . . . I mean as man to . . . [*He hesitates.*]

MANUFACTURER [*waiving the point*]. Yes, yes.

PIERROT. Well, I flatter myself that ...

MANUFACTURER. Exactly. And that's your principal danger. Whilst you are striding along gazing at the stars, you may be treading on a little glow-worm. Shall I give you a third verse for your song?

> " Life's a woman calling,
>   Do not stop your ears,
>   Lest, when night is falling,
>   Darkness brings you tears."

[*The* MANUFACTURER'S *kindly and impressive tone holds* PIERROT *as it had held* PIERRETTE *some moments before. Whilst the two are looking at each other, a little red cloak dances past the window, and* PIERRETTE *enters with her marketing.*

PIERRETTE. Oh, I'm so glad you're still here.

MANUFACTURER. But I must be going now. I am a great traveller.

PIERRETTE [*standing against the door, so that he cannot pass*]. Oh, you mustn't go yet.

MANUFACTURER. Don't make me fly out of the window. I only do that under very unpleasant circumstances.

PIERROT [*gaily, with mock eloquence*]. Pierrette, regard our visitor. You little knew whom you were entertaining. You see before you the maker of the dreams that slip about the world like little fish among the rushes of a stream. He has given me the bill of lading of his great masterpiece, and it only remains for me to find her. [*Dropping to the commonplace*] I wish I knew where to look.

MANUFACTURER. Before I go, I will give you this little rhyme:

> " Let every woman keep a school,
>   For every man is born a fool."

[*He bows, and goes out quickly and silently.*

THE MAKER OF DREAMS

PIERRETTE [*running to the door, and looking out*]. Why, how quickly he has gone! He's out of sight.

PIERROT. At last I am about to attain my great ideal. There will be a grand wedding, and I shall wear my white coat with the silver braid, and carry a tall gold-topped stick. [*Singing*]

" If we play any longer, I fear you will get
Such a cold in the head, for the grass is so wet.
But during the night, Margareta divine,
I will hang the wet grass up to dry on the line."

Pierrette, I feel that I am about to enter into a man's inheritance, a woman's love.

PIERRETTE. I wish you every happiness.

PIERROT [*singing teasingly*].

"We shall meet in our dreams, that's a thing understood;
You dream of the river, I'll dream of the wood.
I am visiting you, if the river it be;
If we meet in the wood, you are visiting me."

PIERRETTE. We must make lots of money, so that you can give her all she wants. I'll dance and dance until I fall, and the people will exclaim, " Why, she has danced herself to death."

PIERROT. You're right. We must pull the show together. I'll do that article for the paper at once.

[*He takes paper, ink, etc., from the dresser, and, seating himself at the table, commences to write.*

" There has lately come to this town a company of strolling players, who give a show that is at once musical and droll. The audience is enthralled by Pierrot's magnificent singing and dancing, and . . . er . . . very much entertained by Pierrette's homely dancing. Pierrette is a charming comedienne of twenty, with . . ." what colour hair ?

PIERRETTE. Fair, quite fair.

PIERROT. Funny how one can see a person every day and not know the colour of their hair. " Fair hair and . . ." eyes?

PIERRETTE. Blue, Pierrot.

PIERROT. " Fair hair and blue eyes." Fair! Blue! Oh, of course it's nonsense, though.

PIERRETTE. What's nonsense?

PIERROT. Something I was thinking. Most girls have fair hair and blue eyes.

PIERRETTE. Yes, Pierrot, we can't all be ideals.

PIERROT. How musical your voice sounds. I can't make it out. Oh, but, of course, it *is* all nonsense! [*He takes the bill of lading from his pocket and reads it.*]

PIERRETTE. What's nonsense? . . . Pierrot, won't you tell me?

PIERROT. Pierrette, stand in the light.

PIERRETTE. Is anything the matter?

PIERROT. I almost believe that nothing matters. [*Reading and glancing at her*] " Eyes that say ' I love you '; arms that say ' I want you '; lips that say ' Why don't you ? ' " Pierrette, is it possible! I've never noticed before how beautiful you are. You don't seem a bit the same. I believe you have lost your real face, and have carved another out of a rose.

PIERRETTE. Oh, Pierrot, what is it?

PIERROT. Love! I've found it at last. Don't you understand it all?

> " I am a fool
>   Who has learned wisdom in your school."

To think that I've seen you every day, and never dreamed . . . dreamed! Yes, ah, yes, it's one of his beautiful dreams That is why my heart seems full of the early morning.

THE MAKER OF DREAMS

PIERRETTE. Ah, Pierrot!

PIERROT. Oh, how my shoulders tingle! I want to soar up, up. Don't you want to fly up to the roof of heaven and sing among the stars?

PIERRETTE. I have been sitting on the moon ever so long, waiting for my lover. Pierrot, let me try on your smile. Give it to me in a kiss.

> [*With their hands outstretched behind them, they lean towards each other, till their lips meet in a long kiss.*

PIERRETTE [*throwing back her head with a deep sigh of happiness*]. Oh, I am so happy. This might be the end of all things.

PIERROT. Pierrette, let us sit by the fire and put our feet on the fender, and live happily ever after.

> [*They have moved slowly to the settle. As they sit there,* PIERROT *sings softly:*

" Baby, don't wait for the moon,
    The stairs of the sky are so steep;
And mellow and musical June
    Is waiting to kiss you to sleep."

> [*The lamp on the hood of the chimneypiece has burned down, leaving only the red glow from the fire upon their faces, as the curtain whispers down to hide them.*

CURTAIN

Permission to perform this play may be obtained on application to Messrs Samuel French, Ltd., 26 Southampton Street, Strand, London, W.C.2, or 28–30 West 38th Street, New York. Copies of the music can also be purchased from the same firm.

THE LITTLE MAN
A FARCICAL MORALITY
IN THREE SCENES
BY JOHN GALSWORTHY

Mr John Galsworthy's most characteristic plays are "The Silver Box," "Justice," and "Strife." In these dramas (as in most of his work) one feels that he is making use of the theatre in order to expose the evils of the time, and also to advocate certain definite reforms. They are written to instruct rather than to amuse. Tragedy and irony are Mr Galsworthy's outstanding qualities, and his plays might be described as sociological dramas of great power. Every one admires the dispassionate and impartial attitude of the author: he compels himself to write calmly and with strict justice whatever may be his private emotions. This artistic restraint on the part of the dramatist adds immeasurably to the strength and effectiveness of his work.

Apart from his plays, Mr John Galsworthy has written a number of novels which reveal the same dignified and inexorable personality, but—one is bound to add—his kindly humour mellows and softens without weakening the strokes. His style is distinguished by a masterful ease.

CHARACTERS

The Little Man
The American
The Englishman
The Englishwoman
The German
The Dutch Boy

The Mother
The Baby
The Waiter
The Station Official
The Policeman
The Porter

THE LITTLE MAN

Scene I: *Afternoon, on the departure platform of an Austrian railway station. At several little tables outside the buffet persons are taking refreshment, served by a pale young waiter. On a seat against the wall of the buffet a woman of lowly station is sitting beside two large bundles, on one of which she has placed her baby, swathed in a black shawl.*

WAITER [*approaching a table whereat sit an English traveller and his wife*]. Two coffee ?

ENGLISHMAN [*paying*]. Thanks. [*To his wife, in an Oxford voice*] Sugar ?

ENGLISHWOMAN [*in a Cambridge voice*]. One.

AMERICAN TRAVELLER [*with field-glasses and a pocket camera—from another table*]. Waiter, I'd like to have you get my eggs. I've been sitting here quite a while.

WAITER. Yes, sare.

GERMAN TRAVELLER. Kellner, bezahlen ! [*His voice is, like his moustache, stiff and brushed up at the ends. His figure also is stiff and his hair a little grey ; clearly once, if not now, a colonel.*]

WAITER. Komm' gleich !

    [*The* BABY *on the bundle wails. The* MOTHER *takes it up to soothe it. A young, red-cheeked Dutchman at the fourth table stops eating and laughs.*

AMERICAN. My eggs ! Get a wiggle on you !

WAITER. Yes, sare. [*He rapidly recedes.*]

[*A* LITTLE MAN *in a soft hat is seen to the right of tables. He stands a moment looking after the hurrying waiter, then seats himself at the fifth table.*

ENGLISHMAN [*looking at his watch*]. Ten minutes more.

ENGLISHWOMAN. Bother!

AMERICAN [*addressing them*]. 'Pears as if they'd a prejudice against eggs here, anyway.

[*The* ENGLISH *look at him, but do not speak.*

GERMAN [*in creditable English*]. In these places man can get nothing.

[*The* WAITER *comes flying back with a compote for the* DUTCH YOUTH, *who pays.*

GERMAN. Kellner, bezahlen!

WAITER. Eine Krone sechzig. [*The* GERMAN *pays.*

AMERICAN [*rising, and taking out his watch—blandly*]. See here. If I don't get my eggs before this watch ticks twenty, there'll be another waiter in heaven.

WAITER [*flying*]. Komm' gleich!

AMERICAN [*seeking sympathy*]. I'm gettin' kind of mad!

[*The* ENGLISHMAN *halves his newspaper and hands the advertisement half to his wife. The* BABY *wails. The* MOTHER *rocks it. The* DUTCH YOUTH *stops eating and laughs. The* GERMAN *lights a cigarette. The* LITTLE MAN *sits motionless, nursing his hat. The* WAITER *comes flying back with the eggs and places them before the* AMERICAN.

AMERICAN [*putting away his watch*]. Good! I don't like trouble. How much?

[*He pays and eats. The* WAITER *stands a moment at the edge of the platform and passes his hand across his brow. The* LITTLE MAN *eyes him and speaks gruffly.*

THE LITTLE MAN

LITTLE MAN. Herr Ober! [*The* WAITER *turns.*] Might I have a glass of beer?

WAITER. Yes, sare.

LITTLE MAN. Thank you very much. [*The* WAITER *goes.*

AMERICAN [*pausing in the deglutition of his eggs—affably*]. Pardon me, sir; I'd like to have you tell me why you called that little bit of a feller "Herr Ober." Reckon you would know what that means? Mr Head Waiter.

LITTLE MAN. Yes, yes.

AMERICAN. I smile.

LITTLE MAN. Oughtn't I to call him that?

GERMAN [*abruptly*]. Nein—Kellner.

AMERICAN. Why, yes! Just "waiter."

> [*The* ENGLISHWOMAN *looks round her paper for a second. The* DUTCH YOUTH *stops eating and laughs. The* LITTLE MAN *gazes from face to face and nurses his hat.*

LITTLE MAN. I didn't want to hurt his feelings.

GERMAN. Gott!

AMERICAN. In my country we're very democratic—but that's quite a proposition.

ENGLISHMAN [*handling coffee-pot, to his wife*]. More?

ENGLISHWOMAN. No, thanks.

GERMAN [*abruptly*]. These fellows—if you treat them in this manner, at once they take liberties. You see, you will not get your beer.

> [*As he speaks the* WAITER *returns, bringing the* LITTLE MAN'S *beer, then retires.*

AMERICAN. That 'pears to be one up to democracy. [*To the* LITTLE MAN] I judge you go in for brotherhood?

LITTLE MAN [*startled*]. Oh, no!

AMERICAN. I take considerable stock in Leo Tolstoi myself. Grand man—grand-souled apparatus. But I guess you've got to pinch those waiters some to make 'em skip. [*To the* ENGLISH, *who have carelessly looked his way for a moment*] You'll appreciate that, the way he acted about my eggs.

[*The* ENGLISH *make faint motions with their chins and avert their eyes.*

[*To the* WAITER, *who is standing at the door of the buffet*] Waiter! Flash of beer—jump, now!

WAITER. Komm' gleich!

GERMAN. Cigarren!

WAITER. Schon! [*He disappears.*

AMERICAN [*affably—to the* LITTLE MAN]. Now, if I don't get that flash of beer quicker'n you got yours, I shall admire.

GERMAN [*abruptly*]. Tolstoi is nothing—nichts! No good! Ha?

AMERICAN [*relishing the approach of argument*]. Well, that is a matter of temperament. Now, I'm all for equality. See that poor woman there—very humble woman—there she sits among us with her baby. Perhaps you'd like to locate her somewhere else?

GERMAN [*shrugging*]. Tolstoi is sentimentalisch. Nietszche is the true philosopher, the only one.

AMERICAN. Well, that's quite in the prospectus—very stimulating party—old Nietch—virgin mind. But give me Leo! [*He turns to the red-cheeked* YOUTH] What do you opine, sir? I guess by your labels you'll be Dutch. Do they read Tolstoi in your country?

[*The* DUTCH YOUTH *laughs.*

AMERICAN. That is a very luminous answer.

GERMAN. Tolstoi is nothing. Man should himself express. He must push—he must be strong.

AMERICAN. That is so. In America we believe in virility; we like a man to expand. But we believe in

THE LITTLE MAN

brotherhood too. We draw the line at niggers; but we aspire. Social barriers and distinctions we've not much use for.

ENGLISHMAN. Do you feel a draught?

ENGLISHWOMAN [*with a shiver of her shoulder toward the* AMERICAN]. I do—rather.

GERMAN. Wait! You are a young people.

AMERICAN. That is so; there are no flies on us. [*To the* LITTLE MAN, *who has been gazing eagerly from face to face*] Say! I'd like to have you give us your sentiments in relation to the duty of man.

> [*The* LITTLE MAN *fidgets, and is about to open his mouth.*

AMERICAN. For example—is it your opinion that we should kill off the weak and diseased, and all that can't jump around?

GERMAN [*nodding*]. Ja, ja! That is coming.

LITTLE MAN [*looking from face to face*]. They might be me. [*The* DUTCH YOUTH *laughs.*

AMERICAN [*reproving him with a look*]. That's true humility. 'Tisn't grammar. Now, here's a proposition that brings it nearer the bone: Would you step out of your way to help them when it was liable to bring you trouble?

GERMAN. Nein, nein! That is stupid.

LITTLE MAN [*eager but wistful*]. I'm afraid not. Of course one wants to—— There was St Francis d'Assisi and St Julien l'Hospitalier, and——

AMERICAN. Very lofty dispositions. Guess they died of them. [*He rises.*] Shake hands, sir—my name is—— [*He hands a card.*] I am an ice-machine maker. [*He shakes the* LITTLE MAN's *hand.*] I like your sentiments—I feel kind of brotherly. [*Catching sight of the* WAITER *appearing in the doorway*] Waiter, where to h—ll is that flash of beer?

GERMAN. Cigarren!

WAITER. Komm' gleich! [*He vanishes.*

ENGLISHMAN [*consulting watch*]. Train's late.

ENGLISHWOMAN. Really! Nuisance!

[*A station* POLICEMAN, *very square and uniformed, passes and repasses.*

AMERICAN [*resuming his seat—to the* GERMAN]. Now, we don't have so much of that in America. Guess we feel more to trust in human nature.

GERMAN. Ah! ha! you will bresently find there is nothing in him but self.

LITTLE MAN [*wistfully*]. Don't you believe in human nature?

AMERICAN. Very stimulating question. [*He looks round for opinions.*] [*The* DUTCH YOUTH *laughs.*

ENGLISHMAN [*holding out his half of the paper to his wife*]. Swap! [*His wife swaps.*

GERMAN. In human nature I believe so far as I can see him—no more.

AMERICAN. Now that 'pears to me kind o' blasphemy. I believe in heroism. I opine there's not one of us settin' around here that's not a hero—give him the occasion.

LITTLE MAN. Oh! Do you believe that?

AMERICAN. Well! I judge a hero is just a person that'll help another at the expense of himself. Take 'that poor woman there. Well, now, she's a heroine, I guess. She would die for her baby any old time.

GERMAN. Animals will die for their babies. That is nothing.

AMERICAN. I carry it further. I postulate we would all die for that baby if a locomotive was to trundle up right here and try to handle it. [*To the* GERMAN] I guess *you* don't know how good you are. [*As the* GERMAN *is twisting up the ends of his moustache—to the*

THE LITTLE MAN

ENGLISHWOMAN] I should like to have you express an opinion, ma'am.

ENGLISHWOMAN. I beg your pardon.

AMERICAN. The English are very humanitarian; they have a very high sense of duty. So have the Germans, so have the Americans. [*To the* DUTCH YOUTH] I judge even in your little country they have that. This is an epoch of equality and high-toned ideals. [*To the* LITTLE MAN] What is *your* nationality, sir?

LITTLE MAN. I'm afraid I'm nothing particular. My father was half-English and half-American, and my mother half-German and half-Dutch.

AMERICAN. My! That's a bit streaky, any old way. [*The* POLICEMAN *passes again.*] Now, I don't believe we've much use any more for those gentlemen in buttons. We've grown kind of mild—we don't think of self as we used to do.   [*The* WAITER *has appeared in the doorway.*

GERMAN [*in a voice of thunder*]. Cigarren! Donnerwetter!

AMERICAN [*shaking his fist at the vanishing* WAITER]. That flash of beer!

WAITER. Komm' gleich!

AMERICAN. A little more, and he will join George Washington! I was about to remark when he intruded: In this year of grace 1913 the kingdom of Christ is quite a going concern. We are mighty near to universal brotherhood. The colonel here [*he indicates the* GERMAN] is a man of blood and iron, but give him an opportunity to be magnanimous, and he'll be right there. Oh, sir! yep!

[*The* GERMAN, *with a profound mixture of pleasure and cynicism, brushes up the ends of his moustache.*

LITTLE MAN. I wonder. One wants to, but somehow—— [*He shakes his head.*]

AMERICAN. You seem kind of skeery about that. You've had experience, maybe. I'm an optimist—I think we're bound to make the devil hum in the near future. I opine we shall occasion a good deal of trouble to that old party. There's about to be a holocaust of selfish interests. The colonel there with old-man Nietch—he won't know himself. There's going to be a very sacred opportunity.

> [*As he speaks, the voice of a* RAILWAY OFFICIAL *is heard in the distance calling out in German. It approaches, and the words become audible.*

GERMAN [*startled*]. Der Teufel! [*He gets up, and seizes the bag beside him.*]

> [*The* STATION OFFICIAL *has appeared; he stands for a moment casting his commands at the seated group. The* DUTCH YOUTH *also rises, and takes his coat and hat. The* OFFICIAL *turns on his heel and retires, still issuing directions.*

ENGLISHMAN. What does he say?

GERMAN. Our drain has come in, de oder platform; only one minute we haf. [*All have risen in a fluster.*

AMERICAN. Now, that's very provoking. I won't get that flash of beer.

> [*There is a general scurry to gather coats and hats and wraps, during which the lowly* WOMAN *is seen making desperate attempts to deal with her baby and the two large bundles. Quite defeated, she suddenly puts all down, wrings her hands, and cries out:* " Herr Jesu! Hilfe! " *The flying procession turn their heads at that strange cry.*

AMERICAN. What's that? Help? [*He continues to run.*

> [*The* LITTLE MAN *spins round, rushes back, picks up baby and bundle on which it was seated.*

THE LITTLE MAN

LITTLE MAN. Come along, good woman, come along!
[*The* WOMAN *picks up the other bundle and they run.*
[*The* WAITER, *appearing in the doorway with the bottle of beer, watches with his tired smile.*

CURTAIN

SCENE II: *A second-class compartment of a corridor carriage, in motion. In it are seated the* ENGLISHMAN *and his* WIFE, *opposite each other at the corridor end, she with her face to the engine, he with his back. Both are somewhat protected from the rest of the travellers by newspapers. Next to her sits the* GERMAN, *and opposite him sits the* AMERICAN; *next the* AMERICAN *in one window corner is seated the* DUTCH YOUTH; *the other window corner is taken by the* GERMAN's *bag. The silence is only broken by the slight rushing noise of the train's progression and the crackling of the English newspapers.*

AMERICAN [*turning to the* DUTCH YOUTH]. Guess I'd like that window raised; it's kind of chilly after that old run they gave us.
[*The* DUTCH YOUTH *laughs, and goes through the motions of raising the window. The* ENGLISH *regard the operation with uneasy irritation. The* GERMAN *opens his bag, which reposes on the corner seat next him, and takes out a book.*
AMERICAN. The Germans are great readers. Very stimulating practice. I read most anything myself!
[*The* GERMAN *holds up the book so that the title may be read.*

Don Quixote—fine book. We Americans take considerable stock in old-man Quixote. Bit of a wild-cat—but we don't laugh at him.

GERMAN. He is dead. Dead as a sheep. A good thing, too.

AMERICAN. In America we have still quite an amount of chivalry.

GERMAN. Chivalry is nothing — sentimentalisch. In modern days—no good. A man must push, he must pull.

AMERICAN. So you say. But I judge your form of chivalry is sacrifice to the State. We allow more freedom to the individual soul. Where there's something little and weak, we feel it kind of noble to give up to it. That way we feel elevated.

> [*As he speaks there is seen in the corridor doorway the* LITTLE MAN, *with the* WOMAN'S BABY *still on his arm and the bundle held in the other hand. He peers in anxiously. The* ENGLISH, *acutely conscious, try to dissociate themselves from his presence with their papers. The* DUTCH YOUTH *laughs.*

GERMAN. Ach! So!

AMERICAN. Dear me!

LITTLE MAN. Is there room? I can't find a seat.

AMERICAN. Why, yes! There's a seat for one.

LITTLE MAN [*depositing bundle outside, and heaving* BABY]. May I?

AMERICAN. Come right in!

> [*The* GERMAN *sulkily moves his bag. The* LITTLE MAN *comes in and seats himself gingerly.*

AMERICAN. Where's the mother?

LITTLE MAN [*ruefully*]. Afraid she got left behind.

> [*The* DUTCH YOUTH *laughs. The* ENGLISH *unconsciously emerge from their newspapers.*

THE LITTLE MAN

AMERICAN. My! That would appear to be quite a domestic incident.

> [*The* ENGLISHMAN *suddenly utters a profound "Ha, ha!" and disappears behind his paper. And that paper and the one opposite are seen to shake, and little squirls and squeaks emerge.*

GERMAN. And you haf got her bundle, and her baby. Ha! [*He cackles drily.*]

AMERICAN [*gravely*]. I smile. I guess Providence has played it pretty low down on you. It's sure acted real mean.

> [*The* BABY *wails, and the* LITTLE MAN *jigs it with a sort of gentle desperation, looking apologetically from face to face. His wistful glance renews the fire of merriment wherever it alights. The* AMERICAN *alone preserves a gravity which seems incapable of being broken.*

AMERICAN. Maybe you'd better get off right smart and restore that baby. There's nothing can act madder than a mother.

LITTLE MAN. Poor thing, yes! What she must be suffering!

> [*A gale of laughter shakes the carriage. The* ENGLISH *for a moment drop their papers, the better to indulge. The* LITTLE MAN *smiles a wintry smile.*

AMERICAN [*in a lull*]. How did it eventuate?

LITTLE MAN. We got there just as the train was going to start; and I jumped, thinking I could help her up. But it moved too quickly, and—and left her.

> [*The gale of laughter blows up again.*

AMERICAN. Guess I'd have thrown the baby out to her.

LITTLE MAN. I was afraid the poor little thing might break.

[*The* BABY *wails; the* LITTLE MAN *heaves it; the gale of laughter blows.*

AMERICAN [*gravely*]. It's highly entertaining—not for the baby. What kind of an old baby is it, anyway? [*He sniffs.*] I judge it's a bit—niffy.

LITTLE MAN. Afraid I've hardly looked at it yet.

AMERICAN. Which end up is it?

LITTLE MAN. Oh! I think the right end. Yes, yes, it is.

AMERICAN. Well, that's something. Maybe you should hold it out of window a bit. Very excitable things, babies!

ENGLISHWOMAN [*galvanized*]. No, no!

ENGLISHMAN [*touching her knee*]. My dear!

AMERICAN. You are right, ma'am. I opine there's a draught out there. This baby is precious. We've all of us got stock in this baby in a manner of speaking. This is a little bit of universal brotherhood. Is it a woman baby?

LITTLE MAN. I—I can only see the top of its head.

AMERICAN. You can't always tell from that. It looks kind of over-wrapped up. Maybe it had better be unbound.

GERMAN. Nein, nein, nein!

AMERICAN. I think you are very likely right, colonel. It might be a pity to unbind that baby. I guess the lady should be consulted in this matter.

ENGLISHWOMAN. Yes, yes, of course—I——

ENGLISHMAN [*touching her*]. Let it be! Little beggar seems all right.

AMERICAN. That would seem only known to Providence at this moment. I judge it might be due to humanity to look at its face.

LITTLE MAN [*gladly*]. It's sucking my finger. There, there—nice little thing—there!

AMERICAN. I would surmise in your leisure moments you have created babies, sir?

THE LITTLE MAN

LITTLE MAN. Oh! no—indeed, no.

AMERICAN. Dear me!—That is a loss. [*Addressing himself to the carriage at large*] I think we may esteem ourselves fortunate to have this little stranger right here with us. Demonstrates what a hold the little and weak have upon us nowadays. The colonel here—a man of blood and iron—there he sits quite ca'm next door to it. [*He sniffs.*] Now, this baby is ruther chastening—that is a sign of grace, in the colonel—that is true heroism.

LITTLE MAN [*faintly*]. I—I can see its face a little now.

[*All bend forward.*

AMERICAN. What sort of a physiognomy has it, anyway?

LITTLE MAN [*still faintly*]. I don't see anything but—but spots.

GERMAN. Oh! Ha! Pfui! [*The* DUTCH YOUTH *laughs.*

AMERICAN. I am told that is not uncommon amongst babies. Perhaps we could have you inform us, ma'am.

ENGLISHWOMAN. Yes, of course—only—what sort of——?

LITTLE MAN. They seem all over its—— [*At the slight recoil of every one*] I feel sure it's—it's quite a good baby underneath.

AMERICAN. That will be ruther difficult to come at. I'm just a bit sensitive. I've very little use for affections of the epidermis.

GERMAN. Pfui! [*He has edged away as far as he can get, and is lighting a big cigar*].

[*The* DUTCH YOUTH *draws his legs back.*

AMERICAN [*also taking a cigar*]. I guess it would be well to fumigate this carriage. Does it suffer, do you think?

LITTLE MAN [*peering*]. Really, I don't—I'm not sure—I know so little about babies. I think it would have a nice expression—if—if it showed.

AMERICAN. Is it kind of boiled looking?

LITTLE MAN. Yes—yes, it is.

AMERICAN [*looking gravely round*]. I judge this baby has the measles.

> [*The* GERMAN *screws himself spasmodically against the arm of the* ENGLISHWOMAN'S *seat.*

ENGLISHWOMAN. Poor little thing! Shall I——?

> [*She half rises.*

ENGLISHMAN [*touching her*]. No, no—— Dash it!

AMERICAN. I honour your emotion, ma'am. It does credit to us all. But I sympathize with your husband too. The measles is a very important pestilence in connection with a grown woman.

LITTLE MAN. It likes my finger awfully. Really, it's rather a sweet baby.

AMERICAN [*sniffing*]. Well, that would appear to be quite a question. About them spots, now? Are they rosy?

LITTLE MAN. No-o; they're dark, almost black.

GERMAN. Gott! Typhus! [*He bounds up on to the arm of the* ENGLISHWOMAN'S *seat.*]

AMERICAN. Typhus! That's quite an indisposition!

> [*The* DUTCH YOUTH *rises suddenly, and bolts out into the corridor. He is followed by the* GERMAN, *puffing clouds of smoke. The* ENGLISH *and* AMERICAN *sit a moment longer without speaking. The* ENGLISHWOMAN'S *face is turned with a curious expression—half pity, half fear—toward the* LITTLE MAN. *Then the* ENGLISHMAN *gets up.*

ENGLISHMAN. Bit stuffy for you here, dear, isn't it?

> [*He puts his arm through hers, raises her, and almost pushes her through the doorway. She goes, still looking back.*

AMERICAN [*gravely*]. There's nothing I admire more'n courage. Guess I'll go and smoke in the corridor.

> [*As he goes out the* LITTLE MAN *looks very wistfully after him. Screwing up his mouth and nose, he*

THE LITTLE MAN

holds the BABY *away from him and wavers; then
rising, he puts it on the seat opposite and goes
through the motions of letting down the window.
Having done so he looks at the* BABY, *who has
begun to wail. Suddenly he raises his hands and
clasps them, like a child praying. Since, however,
the* BABY *does not stop wailing, he hovers over it
in indecision; then, picking it up, sits down
again to dandle it, with his face turned toward the
open window. Finding that it still wails, he
begins to sing to it in a cracked little voice. It
is charmed at once. While he is singing, the*
AMERICAN *appears in the corridor. Letting down
the passage window, he stands there in the doorway
with the draught blowing his hair and the smoke
of his cigar all about him. The* LITTLE MAN *stops
singing and shifts the shawl higher to protect the*
BABY'S *head from the draught.*

AMERICAN [*gravely*]. This is the most sublime spectacle I have ever envisaged. There ought to be a record of this.

                  [*The* LITTLE MAN *looks at him, wondering.*

You are typical, sir, of the sentiments of modern Christianity. You illustrate the deepest feelings in the heart of every man.

      [*The* LITTLE MAN *rises with the* BABY *and a movement of approach.*

Guess I'm wanted in the dining-car.   [*He vanishes.*

      [*The* LITTLE MAN *sits down again, but back to the engine, away from the draught, and looks out of the window, patiently jogging the* BABY *on his knee.*

CURTAIN

SCENE III: *An arrival platform. The* LITTLE MAN, *with the* BABY *and the bundle, is standing disconsolate, while travellers pass and luggage is being carried by. A* STATION OFFICIAL, *accompanied by a* POLICEMAN, *appears from a doorway, behind him.*

OFFICIAL [*consulting telegram in his hand*]. Das ist der Herr.
   [*They advance to the* LITTLE MAN.
OFFICIAL. Sie haben einen Buben gestohlen?
LITTLE MAN. I only speak English and American.
OFFICIAL. Dies ist nicht Ihr Bube? [*He touches the* BABY.
LITTLE MAN [*shaking his head*]. Take care—it's ill.
   [*The man does not understand.*
Ill—the baby——
OFFICIAL [*shaking his head*]. Verstehe nicht. Dis is nod your baby? No?
LITTLE MAN [*shaking his head violently*]. No, it is not. No.
OFFICIAL [*tapping the telegram*]. Gut! You are 'rested.
   [*He signs to the* POLICEMAN, *who takes the* LITTLE MAN'S *arm.*
LITTLE MAN. Why? I don't want the poor baby.
OFFICIAL [*lifting the bundle*]. Dies ist nicht Ihr Gepäck—pag?
LITTLE MAN. No.
OFFICIAL. Gut. You are 'rested.
LITTLE MAN. I only took it for the poor woman. I'm not a thief—I'm—I'm——
OFFICIAL [*shaking head*]. Verstehe nicht.
   [*The* LITTLE MAN *tries to tear his hair. The disturbed* BABY *wails.*
LITTLE MAN [*dandling it as best he can*]. There, there—poor, poor!

THE LITTLE MAN

OFFICIAL. Halt still! You are 'rested. It is all right.

LITTLE MAN. Where is the mother?

OFFICIAL. She komm by next drain. Das telegram say: Halt einen Herrn mit schwarzem Buben und schwarzem Gepäck. 'Rest gentleman mit black baby und black—pag.

[*The* LITTLE MAN *turns up his eyes to heaven.*

OFFICIAL. Komm mit us.

[*They take the* LITTLE MAN *toward the door from which they have come. A voice stops them.*

AMERICAN [*speaking from as far away as may be*]. Just a moment!

[*The* OFFICIAL *stops; the* LITTLE MAN *also stops and sits down on a bench against the wall. The* POLICEMAN *stands stolidly beside him. The* AMERICAN *approaches a step or two, beckoning; the* OFFICIAL *goes up to him.*

AMERICAN. Guess you've got an angel from heaven there! What's the gentleman in buttons for?

OFFICIAL. Was ist das?

AMERICAN. Is there anybody here that can understand American?

OFFICIAL. Verstehe nicht.

AMERICAN. Well, just watch my gestures. I was saying [*he points to the* LITTLE MAN, *then makes gestures of flying*] you have an angel from heaven there. You have there a man in whom Gawd [*he points upward*] takes quite an amount of stock. You have no call to arrest him. [*He makes the gesture of arrest.*] No, sir. Providence has acted pretty mean, loading off that baby on him. [*He makes the motion of dandling.*] The little man has a heart of gold. [*He points to his heart, and takes out a gold coin.*]

OFFICIAL [*thinking he is about to be bribed*]. Aber, das ist zu viel!

AMERICAN. Now, don't rattle me! [*Pointing to the*

LITTLE MAN] Man [*pointing to his heart*] Herz [*pointing to the coin*] von Gold. This is a flower of the field—he don't want no gentleman in buttons to pluck him up.

> [*A little crowd is gathering, including the* TWO ENGLISH, *the* GERMAN, *and the* DUTCH YOUTH.

OFFICIAL. Verstehe absolut nichts. [*He taps the telegram.*] Ich muss mein duty do.

AMERICAN. But I'm telling you. This is a white man. This is probably the whitest man on Gawd's earth.

OFFICIAL. Das macht nichts—gut or no gut, I muss mein duty do. [*He turns to go toward the* LITTLE MAN.]

AMERICAN. Oh! Very well, arrest him; do your duty. This baby has typhus.

> [*At the word "typhus" the* OFFICIAL *stops.*

AMERICAN [*making gestures*]. First-class typhus, black typhus, schwarzen typhus. Now you have it. I'm kind o' sorry for you and the gentleman in buttons. Do your duty!

OFFICIAL. Typhus? Der Bub'—die baby hat typhus?

AMERICAN. I'm telling you.

OFFICIAL. Gott im Himmel!

AMERICAN [*spotting the* GERMAN *in the little throng*]. Here's a gentleman will corroborate me.

OFFICIAL [*much disturbed, and signing to the* POLICEMAN *to stand clear*]. Typhus! Aber das ist grässlich!

AMERICAN. I kind o' thought you'd feel like that.

OFFICIAL. Die Sanitätsmachine! Gleich!

> [*A* PORTER *goes to get it. From either side the broken half-moon of persons stand gazing at the* LITTLE MAN, *who sits unhappily dandling the* BABY *in the centre.*

OFFICIAL [*raising his hands*]. Was zu thun?

AMERICAN. Guess you'd better isolate the baby.

THE LITTLE MAN

[*A silence, during which the* LITTLE MAN *is heard faintly whistling and clucking to the* BABY.

OFFICIAL [*referring once more to his telegram*]. " 'Rest gentleman mit black baby." [*Shaking his head*] Wir must de gentleman hold. [*To the* GERMAN] Bitte, mein Herr, sagen Sie ihm, den Buben zu niedersetzen. [*He makes the gesture of deposit.*]

GERMAN [*to the* LITTLE MAN]. He say: Put down the baby.

[*The* LITTLE MAN *shakes his head, and continues to dandle the* BABY.

OFFICIAL. You must.

[*The* LITTLE MAN *glowers in silence.*

ENGLISHMAN [*in background—muttering*]. Good man!

GERMAN. His spirit ever denies.

OFFICIAL [*again making his gesture*]. Aber er muss!

[*The* LITTLE MAN *makes a face at him.*

Sag' ihm: Instantly put down baby, and komm mit us.

[*The* BABY *wails.*

LITTLE MAN. Leave the poor ill baby here alone? Be—be—be d——d to you!

AMERICAN [*jumping on to a trunk—with enthusiasm*]. Bully!

[*The* ENGLISH *clap their hands; the* DUTCH YOUTH *laughs. The* OFFICIAL *is muttering, greatly incensed.*

AMERICAN. What does that body-snatcher say?

GERMAN. He say this man use the baby to save himself from arrest. Very smart—he say.

AMERICAN. I judge you do him an injustice. [*Showing off the* LITTLE MAN *with a sweep of his arm*] This is a white man. He's got a black baby, and he won't leave it in the lurch. Guess we would all act noble, that way, give us the chance

[*The* LITTLE MAN *rises, holding out the* BABY, *and advances a step or two. The half-moon at once gives, increasing its size; the* AMERICAN *climbs on to a higher trunk. The* LITTLE MAN *retires and again sits down.*

AMERICAN [*addressing the* OFFICIAL]. Guess you'd better go out of business and wait for the mother.

OFFICIAL [*stamping his foot*]. Die Mutter sall 'rested be for taking out baby mit typhus. Ha! [*To the* LITTLE MAN] Put ze baby down!   [*The* LITTLE MAN *smiles.* Do you 'ear?

AMERICAN [*addressing the* OFFICIAL]. Now, see here. 'Pears to me you don't suspicion just how beautiful this is. Here we have a man giving his life for that old baby that's got no claim on him. This is not a baby of his own making. No, sir, this is a very Christ-like proposition in the gentleman.

OFFICIAL. Put ze baby down, or ich will gommand some one it to do.

AMERICAN. That will be very interesting to watch.

OFFICIAL [*to* POLICEMAN]. Dake it vrom him.

      [*The* POLICEMAN *mutters, but does not.*

AMERICAN [*to the* GERMAN]. Guess I lost that.

GERMAN. He say he is not his officier.

AMERICAN. That just tickles me to death.

OFFICIAL [*looking round*]. Vill nobody dake ze Bub'?

ENGLISHWOMAN [*moving a step—faintly*]. Yes—I——

ENGLISHMAN [*grasping her arm*]. By Jove! Will you!

OFFICIAL [*gathering himself for a great effort to take the* BABY, *and advancing two steps*]. Zen I gommand you—— [*He stops and his voice dies away.*] Zit dere!

AMERICAN. My! That's wonderful. What a man this is! What a sublime sense of duty!

     [*The* DUTCH YOUTH *laughs. The* OFFICIAL *turns on*

THE LITTLE MAN

him, but as he does so the MOTHER *of the* BABY *is seen hurrying.*

MOTHER. Ach! Ach! Mei' Bubi!

   [*Her face is illumined; she is about to rush to the* LITTLE MAN.

OFFICIAL [*to the* POLICEMAN]. Nimm die Frau!

   [*The* POLICEMAN *catches hold of the* WOMAN.

OFFICIAL [*to the frightened* WOMAN]. Warum haben Sie einen Buben mit Typhus mit ausgebracht?

AMERICAN [*eagerly, from his perch*]. What was that? I don't want to miss any.

GERMAN. He say: Why did you a baby with typhus with you bring out?

AMERICAN. Well, that's quite a question.

   [*He takes out the field-glasses slung around him and adjusts them on the* BABY.

MOTHER [*bewildered*]. Mei' Bubi—Typhus—aber Typhus? [*She shakes her head violently.*] Nein, nein, nein! Typhus!

OFFICIAL. Er hat Typhus.

MOTHER [*shaking her head*]. Nein, nein, nein!

AMERICAN [*looking through his glasses*]. Guess she's kind of right! I judge the typhus is where the baby's slobbered on the shawl, and it's come off on him.

   [*The* DUTCH YOUTH *laughs.*

OFFICIAL [*turning on him furiously*]. Er hat Typhus.

AMERICAN. Now, that's where you slop over. Come right here.

   [*The* OFFICIAL *mounts, and looks through the glasses.*

AMERICAN [*to the* LITTLE MAN]. Skin out the baby's leg. If we don't locate spots on that, it'll be good enough for me.

   [*The* LITTLE MAN *fumbles out the* BABY'S *little white foot.*

MOTHER. Mei' Bubi! [*She tries to break away.*]

131

AMERICAN. White as a banana. [*To the* OFFICIAL—*affably*] Guess you've made kind of a fool of us with your old typhus.

OFFICIAL. Lass die Frau!

[*The* POLICEMAN *lets her go, and she rushes to her* BABY.

MOTHER. Mei' Bubi!

[*The* BABY, *exchanging the warmth of the* LITTLE MAN *for the momentary chill of its* MOTHER, *wails.*

OFFICIAL [*descending and beckoning to the* POLICEMAN]. Sie wollen den Herrn accusiren?

[*The* POLICEMAN *takes the* LITTLE MAN'S *arm.*

AMERICAN. What's that? They goin' to pinch him after all?

[*The* MOTHER, *still hugging her* BABY, *who has stopped crying, gazes at the* LITTLE MAN, *who sits dazedly looking up. Suddenly she drops on her knees, and with her free hand lifts his booted foot and kisses it.*

AMERICAN [*waving his hat*]. Ra! Ra! [*He descends swiftly, goes up to the* LITTLE MAN, *whose arm the* POLICEMAN *has dropped, and takes his hand.*] Brother, I am proud to know you. This is one of the greatest moments I have ever experienced. [*Displaying the* LITTLE MAN *to the assembled company*] I think I sense the situation when I say that we all esteem it an honour to breathe the rather inferior atmosphere of this station here along with our little friend. I guess we shall all go home and treasure the memory of his face as the whitest thing in our museum of recollections. And perhaps this good woman will also go home and wash the face of our little brother here. I am inspired with a new faith in mankind. Ladies and gentlemen, I wish to present to you a sure-enough saint—only wants a halo, to be transfigured. [*To the* LITTLE MAN] Stand right up.

THE LITTLE MAN

[*The* LITTLE MAN *stands up bewildered. They come about him. The* OFFICIAL *bows to him, the* POLICEMAN *salutes him. The* DUTCH YOUTH *shakes his head and laughs. The* GERMAN *draws himself up very straight, and bows quickly twice. The* ENGLISHMAN *and his* WIFE *approach at least two steps, then, thinking better of it, turn to each other and recede. The* MOTHER *kisses his hand. The* PORTER, *returning with the Sanitätsmachine, turns it on from behind, and its pinkish shower, goldened by a ray of sunlight, falls around the* LITTLE MAN'S *head, transfiguring it as he stands with eyes upraised to see whence the portent comes.*

AMERICAN [*rushing forward and dropping on his knees*]. Hold on just a minute! Guess I'll take a snapshot of the miracle. [*He adjusts his pocket camera.*] This ought to look bully!

CURTAIN

Applications regarding amateur performances of this play should be addressed to The Authors' Society, 1 Central Buildings, Tothill Street, Westminster, London, S.W.1, or to Messrs Curtis Brown, Ltd., Knickerbocker Theatre Building, New York.

A NIGHT AT AN INN
A PLAY IN ONE ACT
By Lord Dunsany

LORD DUNSANY comes of an old Irish family. In fact, his name and ancestry are said to be the third oldest in Irish history. He succeeded to his title and estates when he was twenty-one.

Lord Dunsany joined the Army and fought in the South African War, but (like Mr A. A. Milne) he spent his leisure as a professional soldier in writing stories and plays. His first book was published when he was twenty-seven, and his first play performed four years later.

He fought in the European War, as lieutenant in the 1st Battalion of the Coldstream Guards, and as captain in the Royal Inniskilling Fusiliers. He was wounded in 1916.

Lord Dunsany's command over language is wonderful: it is the English of Bunyan and the Bible. He has extraordinary inventiveness in Oriental nomenclature. The keynote of his style is the fantastic—in the imaginative sense of the word. His most recent book (1924) is entitled *The King of Elfland's Daughter*.

The play "A Night at an Inn" was written at a single sitting.

Lord Dunsany's chief dramatic works include the following: "The Glittering Gate," "The Gods of the Mountain," "The Golden Doom," "The Laughter of the Gods," "A Good Bargain," and, most remarkable of all (so far), "If."

CHARACTERS

A. E. SCOTT-FORTESCUE (THE TOFF), *a dilapidated gentleman*
WILLIAM JONES (BILL) ⎫
ALBERT THOMAS ⎬ *merchant sailors*
JACOB SMITH (SNIGGERS) ⎭
FIRST PRIEST OF KLESH
SECOND PRIEST OF KLESH
THIRD PRIEST OF KLESH
KLESH

This play was first performed April 22, 1916, at the Neighborhood Playhouse, New York.

A NIGHT AT AN INN

The curtain rises on a room in an inn. SNIGGERS *and* BILL *are talking,* THE TOFF *is reading a paper.* ALBERT *sits a little apart.*

SNIGGERS. What's his idea, I wonder?
BILL. I don't know.
SNIGGERS. And how much longer will he keep us here?
BILL. We've been here three days.
SNIGGERS. And 'aven't seen a soul.
BILL. And a pretty penny it cost us when he rented the pub.
SNIGGERS. 'Ow long did 'e rent the pub for?
BILL. You never know with him.
SNIGGERS. It's lonely enough.
BILL. 'Ow long did you rent the pub for, Toffy?
   [THE TOFF *continues to read a sporting paper; he takes no notice of what is said.*
SNIGGERS. E's *such* a toff.
BILL. Yet 'e's clever, no mistake.
SNIGGERS. Those clever ones are the beggars to make a muddle. Their plans are clever enough, but they don't work, and then they make a mess of things much worse than you or me.
BILL. Ah!
SNIGGERS. I don't like this place.
BILL. Why not?
SNIGGERS. I don't like the looks of it.
BILL. He's keeping us here because here those niggers

can't find us. The three heathen priests what was looking for us so. But we want to go and sell our ruby soon.

ALBERT. There's no sense in it.

BILL. Why not, Albert?

ALBERT. Because I gave those black devils the slip in Hull.

BILL. You give 'em the slip, Albert?

ALBERT. The slip, all three of them. The fellows with the gold spots on their foreheads. I had the ruby then and I give them the slip in Hull.

BILL. How did you do it, Albert?

ALBERT. I had the ruby and they were following me . . .

BILL. Who told them you had the ruby? You didn't show it.

ALBERT. No. . . . But they kind of know.

SNIGGERS. They kind of know, Albert?

ALBERT. Yes, they know if you've got it. Well, they sort of mouched after me, and I tells a policeman and he says, O, they were only three poor niggers and they wouldn't hurt me. Ugh! When I thought of what they did in Malta to poor old Jim.

BILL. Yes, and to George in Bombay before we started.

SNIGGERS. Ugh!

BILL. Why didn't you give 'em in charge?

ALBERT. What about the ruby, Bill?

BILL. Ah!

ALBERT. Well, I did better than that. I walks up and down through Hull. I walks slow enough. And then I turns a corner and I runs. I never sees a corner but I turns it. But sometimes I let a corner pass just to fool them. I twists about like a hare. Then I sits down and waits. No priests.

SNIGGERS. What?

ALBERT. No heathen black devils with gold spots on their face. I give 'em the slip.

A NIGHT AT AN INN

BILL. Well done, Albert!

SNIGGERS [*after a sigh of content*]. Why didn't you tell us?

ALBERT. 'Cause 'e won't let you speak. 'E's got 'is plans and 'e thinks we're silly folk. Things must be done 'is way. And all the time I've give 'em the slip. Might 'ave 'ad one o' them crooked knives in him before now but for me who give 'em the slip in Hull.

BILL. Well done, Albert! Do you hear that, Toffy? Albert has give 'em the slip.

THE TOFF. Yes, I hear.

SNIGGERS. Well, what do you say to that?

THE TOFF. Oh! . . . Well done, Albert!

ALBERT. And what a' you going to do?

THE TOFF. Going to wait.

ALBERT. Don't seem to know what 'e's waiting for.

SNIGGERS. It's a nasty place.

ALBERT. It's getting silly, Bill. Our money's gone and we want to sell the ruby. Let's get on to a town.

BILL. But 'e won't come.

ALBERT. Then we'll leave him.

SNIGGERS. We'll be all right if we keep away from Hull.

ALBERT. We'll go to London.

BILL. But 'e must 'ave 'is share.

SNIGGERS. All right. Only let's go. [*To* THE TOFF] We're going, do you hear? Give us the ruby.

THE TOFF. Certainly. [*He gives them a ruby from his waistcoat pocket; it is the size of a small hen's egg. He goes on reading his paper.*]

ALBERT. Come on, Sniggers.

[*Exeunt* ALBERT *and* SNIGGERS.

BILL. Good-bye, old man. We'll give you your fair share, but there's nothing to do here—no girls, no halls, and we must sell the ruby.

THE TOFF. I'm not a fool, Bill.

BILL. No, no, of course not. Of course you ain't, and you've helped us a lot. Good-bye. You'll say good-bye?

THE TOFF. Oh, yes. Good-bye. [*Still reads his paper. Exit* BILL. THE TOFF *puts a revolver on the table beside him and goes on with his papers. After a moment the three men come rushing in again, frightened.*]

SNIGGERS [*out of breath*]. We've come back, Toffy.

THE TOFF. So you have.

ALBERT. Toffy. . . . How did they get here?

THE TOFF. They walked, of course.

ALBERT. But it's eighty miles.

SNIGGERS. Did you know they were here, Toffy?

THE TOFF. Expected them about now.

ALBERT. Eighty miles!

BILL. Toffy, old man . . . what are we to do?

THE TOFF. Ask Albert.

BILL. If they can do things like this, there's no one can save us but you, Toffy. . . . I always knew you were a clever one. We won't be fools any more. We'll obey you, Toffy.

THE TOFF. You're brave enough and strong enough. There isn't many that would steal a ruby eye out of an idol's head, and such an idol as that was to look at, and on such a night. You're brave enough, Bill. But you're all three of you fools. Jim would have none of my plans, and where's Jim? And George. What did they do to him?

SNIGGERS. Don't, Toffy!

THE TOFF. Well, then, your strength is no use to you. You want cleverness; or they'll have you the way they had George and Jim.

ALL. Ugh!

THE TOFF. Those black priests would follow you round

A NIGHT AT AN INN

the world in circles. Year after year, till they got the idol's eye. And if we died with it, they'd follow our grandchildren. That fool thinks he can escape from men like that by running round three streets in the town of Hull.

ALBERT. God's truth, *you* 'aven't escaped them, because they're '*ere*.

THE TOFF. So I supposed.

ALBERT. You *supposed*!

THE TOFF. Yes, I believe there's no announcement in the Society papers. But I took this country seat especially to receive them. There's plenty of room if you dig, it is pleasantly situated, and, what is more important, it is in a very quiet neighbourhood. So I am at home to them this afternoon.

BILL. Well, *you're* a deep one.

THE TOFF. And remember, you've only my wits between you and death, and don't put your futile plans against those of an educated gentleman.

ALBERT. If you're a gentleman, why don't you go about among gentlemen instead of the likes of us?

THE TOFF. Because I was too clever for them as I am too clever for you.

ALBERT. Too clever for them?

THE TOFF. I never lost a game of cards in my life.

BILL. You never lost a game?

THE TOFF. Not when there was money in it.

BILL. Well, well!

THE TOFF. Have a game of poker?

ALL. No, thanks.

THE TOFF. Then do as you're told.

BILL. All right, Toffy.

SNIGGERS. I saw something just then. Hadn't we better draw the curtains?

THE TOFF. No.

SNIGGERS. What?

THE TOFF. Don't draw the curtains.

SNIGGERS. Oh, all right.

BILL. But, Toffy, they can see us. One doesn't let the enemy do that. I don't see why . . .

THE TOFF. No, of course you don't.

BILL. Oh, all right, Toffy.

[*All begin to pull out revolvers.*

THE TOFF [*putting his own away*]. No revolvers, please.

ALBERT. Why not?

THE TOFF. Because I don't want any noise at my party. We might get guests that hadn't been invited. *Knives* are a different matter.

[*All draw knives.* THE TOFF *signs to them not to draw them yet.* TOFFY *has already taken back his ruby.*

BILL. I think they're coming, Toffy.

THE TOFF. Not yet.

ALBERT. When will they come?

THE TOFF. When I am quite ready to receive them. Not before.

SNIGGERS. I should like to get this over.

THE TOFF. Should you? Then we'll have them now.

SNIGGERS. Now?

THE TOFF. Yes. Listen to me. You shall do as you see me do. You will all pretend to go out. I'll show you how. I've got the ruby. When they see me alone they will come for their idol's eye.

BILL. How can they tell like this which of us has it?

THE TOFF. I confess I don't know, but they seem to.

SNIGGERS. What will you do when they come in?

THE TOFF. I shall do nothing.

SNIGGERS. What?

THE TOFF. They will creep up behind me. Then, my

A NIGHT AT AN INN

friends, Sniggers and Bill and Albert, who gave them the slip, will do what they can.

BILL. All right, Toffy. Trust us.

THE TOFF. If you're a little slow, you will see enacted the cheerful spectacle that accompanied the demise of Jim.

SNIGGERS. Don't, Toffy. We'll be there, all right.

THE TOFF. Very well. Now watch me. [*He goes past the windows to the inner door R. He opens it inwards, then, under cover of the open door, he slips down on his knee and closes it, remaining on the inside, appearing to have gone out. He signs to the others, who understand. Then he appears to re-enter in the same manner.*]

THE TOFF. Now, I shall sit with my back to the door. You go out one by one, so far as our friends can make out. Crouch very low to be on the safe side. They mustn't see you through the window. [BILL *makes his sham exit.*

THE TOFF. Remember, no revolvers. The police are, I believe, proverbially inquisitive.

> [*The other two follow* BILL. *All three are now crouching inside the door R.* THE TOFF *puts the ruby beside him on the table. He lights a cigarette. The door at the back opens so slowly that you can hardly say at what moment it began.* THE TOFF *picks up his paper. A native of India wriggles along the floor ever so slowly, seeking cover from chairs. He moves L., where* THE TOFF *is. The three sailors are R.* SNIGGERS *and* ALBERT *lean forward.* BILL'S *arm keeps them back. An armchair had better conceal them from the Indian. The black* PRIEST *nears* THE TOFF. BILL *watches to see if any more are coming. Then he leaps forward alone—he has taken his boots off—and*

knifes the PRIEST. *The* PRIEST *tries to shout, but* BILL's *left hand is over his mouth.* THE TOFF *continues to read his sporting paper. He never looks around.*

BILL [*sotto voce*]. There's only one, Toffy. What shall we do?

THE TOFF [*without turning his head*]. Only one?

BILL. Yes.

THE TOFF. Wait a moment. Let me think. [*Still apparently absorbed in his paper*] Ah, yes. You go back, Bill. We must attract another guest. . . . Now, are you ready?

BILL. Yes.

THE TOFF. All right. You shall now see my demise at my Yorkshire residence. You must receive guests for me. [*He leaps up in full view of the window, flings up both arms and falls to the floor near the dead* PRIEST.] Now, be ready. [*His eyes close. There is a long pause. Again the door opens, very, very slowly. Another* PRIEST *creeps in. He has three golden spots upon his forehead. He looks round, then he creeps up to his companion and turns him over and looks inside of his clenched hands. Then he looks at the recumbent* TOFF. *Then he creeps towards him.* BILL *slips after him and knifes him like the other with his left hand over his mouth.*]

BILL [*sotto voce*]. We've only got two, Toffy.

THE TOFF. Still another.

BILL. What'll we do?

THE TOFF [*sitting up*]. Hum.

BILL. This is the best way, much.

THE TOFF. Out of the question. Never play the same game twice.

BILL. Why not, Toffy?

THE TOFF. Doesn't work if you do.

A NIGHT AT AN INN

BILL. Well?

THE TOFF. I have it, Albert. You will now walk into the room. I showed you how to do it.

ALBERT. Yes.

THE TOFF. Just run over here and have a fight at this window with these two men.

ALBERT. But they're . . .

THE TOFF. Yes, they're dead, my perspicuous Albert. But Bill and I are going to resuscitate them. . . . Come on. [BILL *picks up a body under the arms.*]

THE TOFF. That's right, Bill. [*Does the same.*] Come and help us, Sniggers. . . . [SNIGGERS *comes.*] Keep low, keep low. Wave their arms about, Sniggers. Don't show yourself. Now, Albert, over you go. Our Albert is slain. Back you get, Bill. Back, Sniggers. Still, Albert. Mustn't move when he comes. Not a muscle.

> [*A face appears at the window and stays for some time. Then the door opens and, looking craftily round, the third* PRIEST *enters. He looks at his companions' bodies and turns round. He suspects something. He takes up one of the knives and with a knife in each hand he puts his back to the wall. He looks to the left and right.*]

THE TOFF. Come on, Bill. [*The* PRIEST *rushes to the door.* THE TOFF *knifes the last* PRIEST *from behind.*]

THE TOFF. A good day's work, my friends.

BILL. Well done, Toffy. Oh, you are a deep one!

ALBERT. A deep one if ever there was one.

SNIGGERS. There ain't any more, Bill, are there?

THE TOFF. No more in the world, my friend.

BILL. Aye, that's all there are. There were only three in the temple. Three priests and their beastly idol.

ALBERT. What is it worth, Toffy? Is it worth a thousand pounds?

THE TOFF. It's worth all they've got in the shop. Worth just whatever we like to ask for it.

ALBERT. Then we're millionaires now.

THE TOFF. Yes, and, what is more important, we no longer have any heirs.

BILL. We'll have to sell it now.

ALBERT. That won't be easy. It's a pity it isn't small, and we had half a dozen. Hadn't the idol any other on him?

BILL. No, he was green jade all over and only had this one eye. He had it in the middle of his forehead and was a long sight uglier than anything else in the world.

SNIGGERS. I'm sure we ought all to be very grateful to Toffy.

BILL. And, indeed, we ought.

ALBERT. If it hadn't been for him . . .

BILL. Yes, if it hadn't been for old Toffy . . .

SNIGGERS. He's a deep one.

THE TOFF. Well, you see I just have a knack of foreseeing things.

SNIGGERS. I should think you did.

BILL. Why, I don't suppose anything happens that our Toff doesn't foresee. Does it, Toffy?

THE TOFF. Well, I don't think it does, Bill. I don't think it often does.

BILL. Life is no more than just a game of cards to our old Toff.

THE TOFF. Well, we've taken these fellows' tricks.

SNIGGERS [*going to the window*]. It wouldn't do for anyone to see them.

THE TOFF. Oh, nobody will come this way. We're all alone on a moor.

BILL. Where will we put them?

THE TOFF. Bury them in the cellar, but there's no hurry.

A NIGHT AT AN INN

BILL. And what then, Toffy?

THE TOFF. Why, then we'll go to London and upset the ruby business. We have really come through this job very nicely.

BILL. I think the first thing that we ought to do is to give a little supper to old Toffy. We'll bury these fellows to-night.

ALBERT. Yes, let's.

SNIGGERS. The very thing!

BILL. And we'll all drink his health.

ALBERT. Good old Toffy!

SNIGGERS. He ought to have been a general or a premier. [*They get bottles from cupboard, etc.*]

THE TOFF. Well, we've earned our bit of a supper. [*They sit down.*]

BILL [*glass in hand*]. Here's to old Toffy, who guessed everything!

ALBERT *and* SNIGGERS. Good old Toffy!

BILL. Toffy, who saved our lives and made our fortunes.

ALBERT *and* SNIGGERS. Hear! Hear!

THE TOFF. And here's to Bill, who saved me twice to-night.

BILL. Couldn't have done it but for your cleverness, Toffy.

SNIGGERS. Hear, hear! Hear, hear!

ALBERT. He foresees everything.

BILL. A speech, Toffy. A speech from our general.

ALL. Yes, a speech.

SNIGGERS. A speech.

THE TOFF. Well, get me some water. This whisky's too much for my head, and I must keep it clear till our friends are safe in the cellar.

BILL. Water? Yes, of course. Get him some water, Sniggers.

SNIGGERS. We don't use water here. Where shall I get it?

BILL. Outside in the garden. [*Exit* SNIGGERS.

ALBERT. Here's to future!

BILL. Here's to Albert Thomas, Esquire.

ALBERT. And William Jones, Esquire.

Re-enter SNIGGERS, *terrified*

THE TOFF. Hullo, here's Jacob Smith, Esquire, J.P., *alias* Sniggers, back again.

SNIGGERS. Toffy, I've been thinking about my share in that ruby. I don't want it, Toffy; I don't want it.

THE TOFF. Nonsense, Sniggers. Nonsense.

SNIGGERS. You shall have it, Toffy, you shall have it yourself, only say Sniggers has no share in this 'ere ruby. Say it, Toffy, say it!

BILL. Want to turn informer, Sniggers?

SNIGGERS. No, no. Only I don't want the ruby, Toffy. . . .

THE TOFF. No more nonsense, Sniggers. We're all in together in this. If one hangs, we all hang; but they won't outwit me. Besides, it's not a hanging affair, they had their knives.

SNIGGERS. Toffy, Toffy, I always treated you fair, Toffy. I was always one to say, " Give Toffy a chance." Take back my share, Toffy.

THE TOFF. What's the matter? What are you driving at?

SNIGGERS. Take it back, Toffy.

THE TOFF. Answer me, what are you up to?

SNIGGERS. I don't want my share any more.

BILL. Have you seen the police? [ALBERT *pulls out his knife.*]

THE TOFF. No, no knives, Albert.

ALBERT. What then?

A NIGHT AT AN INN

THE TOFF. The honest truth in open court, barring the ruby. We were attacked.

SNIGGERS. There's no police.

THE TOFF. Well, then, what's the matter?

BILL. Out with it.

SNIGGERS. I swear to God . . .

ALBERT. Well?

THE TOFF. Don't interrupt.

SNIGGERS. I swear I saw something *what I didn't like.*

THE TOFF. What you didn't like?

SNIGGERS [*in tears*]. Oh, Toffy, Toffy, take it back. Take my share. Say you take it.

THE TOFF. What has he seen?

> [*Dead silence, only broken by* SNIGGERS' *sobs. Then steps are heard. Enter a hideous idol. It is blind and gropes its way. It gropes its way to the ruby and picks it up and screws it into a socket in the forehead.* SNIGGERS *still weeps softly, the rest stare in horror. The idol steps out, not groping. Its steps move off, then stop.*

THE TOFF. O, great heavens!

ALBERT [*in a childish, plaintive voice*]. What is it, Toffy?

BILL. Albert, it is that obscene idol [*in a whisper*] come from India.

ALBERT. It is gone.

BILL. It has taken its eye.

SNIGGERS. We are saved.

A VOICE OFF [*with outlandish accent*]. Meestaire William Jones, Able Seaman.

> [THE TOFF *has never spoken, never moved. He only gazes stupidly in horror.*

BILL. Albert, Albert, what is this? [*He rises and walks*

out. One moan is heard. SNIGGERS *goes to the window. He falls back sickly.*]

ALBERT [*in a whisper*]. What has happened?

SNIGGERS. I have seen it. I have seen it. Oh, I have seen it! [*He returns to table.*]

THE TOFF [*laying his hand very gently on* SNIGGERS' *arm, speaking softly and winningly*]. What was it, Sniggers?

SNIGGERS. I have seen it.

ALBERT. What?

SNIGGERS. Oh!

VOICE. Meestaire Albert Thomas, Able Seaman.

ALBERT. Must I go, Toffy? Toffy, must I go?

SNIGGERS [*clutching him*]. Don't move.

ALBERT [*going*]. Toffy, Toffy. [*Exit.*

VOICE. Meestaire Jacob Smith, Able Seaman.

SNIGGERS. I can't go, Toffy, I can't go. I can't do it. [*He goes.*

VOICE. Meestaire Arnold Everett Scott-Fortescue, late Esquire, Able Seaman.

THE TOFF. I did not foresee it. [*Exit.*

CURTAIN

Applications for permission to perform this play should be addressed to Messrs Curtis Brown, Ltd., 6 Henrietta Street, Covent Garden, London, W.C.2, or to the Neighborhood Playhouse, 466 Grand Street, New York.

CAMPBELL OF KILMHOR
A PLAY IN ONE ACT
By J. A. Ferguson

Mr J. A. Ferguson, examples of whose dramatic work have recently been produced at the Birmingham Repertory Theatre, the Court Theatre, and (in an Irish translation) at the Abbey Theatre, Dublin, derived his impulse to play-writing from his connexion with the Glasgow Repertory Theatre. In his plays as in his novels, in " The Scarecrow " and the grim " King of Morven " as well as in *Stealthy Terror* and *The Dark Geraldine*, an atmosphere is at once developed which excites and holds an almost breathless suspense. His appeal to the imagination is always strong, and what the critic of *The Times Literary Supplement* said of his poems—that he was a poet who saw his own visions and found his own inspirations—is in its degree true of all his work.

" Campbell of Kilmhor " is a remarkably interesting play. As every one will admit, it reads very well; but it ' acts ' even better—which is what a good play should always do.

CHARACTERS

Mary Stewart
Morag Cameron
Dugald Stewart
Captain Sandeman
Archibald Campbell
James Mackenzie

This play was first produced by the Scottish Repertory Theatre Company at the Royalty Theatre, Glasgow, on Monday, March 23, 1914, with the following cast:

Mary Stewart . . .	Agnes Lowson
Morag Cameron . .	Rita Thom
Dugald Stewart . .	Nicholas Hannen
Captain Sandeman .	N. N. Wimbush
Archibald Campbell	W. S. Hartford
James Mackenzie .	C. Stewart Robertson

The play produced by Mr Lewis Casson.

CAMPBELL OF KILMHOR

SCENE: *Interior of a lonely cottage on the road from Struan to Rannoch, in North Perthshire.*

TIME: *After the Rising of '45.*

MORAG *is restlessly moving backwards and forwards. The old woman is seated on a low stool beside the peat fire in the centre of the floor.*

The room is scantily furnished and the women are poorly clad. MORAG *is barefooted. At the back is the door that leads to the outside. On the left of the door is a small window. On the right side of the room there is a door that opens into a barn.* MORAG *stands for a moment at the window, looking out.*

MORAG. It is the wild night outside.

MARY STEWART. Is the snow still coming down?

MORAG. It is that then—dancing and swirling with the wind too, and never stopping at all. Aye, and so black I cannot see the other side of the road.

MARY STEWART. That is good.

[MORAG *moves across the floor and stops irresolutely. She is restless, expectant.*

MORAG. Will I be putting the light in the window?

MARY STEWART. Why should you be doing that! You have not heard his call [*turns eagerly*], have you?

MORAG [*with sign of head*]. No, but the light in the window would show him all is well.

MARY STEWART. It would not then! The light was to be put there *after* we had heard the signal.

MORAG. But on a night like this he may have been calling for long and we never hear him.

MARY STEWART. Do not be so anxious, Morag. Keep to what he says. Put more peat on the fire now and sit down.

MORAG [*with increasing excitement*]. I canna, I canna! There is that in me that tells me something is going to befall us this night. Oh, that wind, hear to it, sobbing round the house as if it brought some poor lost soul up to the door, and we refusing it shelter.

MARY STEWART. Do not be fretting yourself like that. Do as I bid you. Put more peats to the fire.

MORAG [*at the wicker peat-basket*]. Never since I . . . What was that? [*Both listen for a moment.*

MARY STEWART. It was just the wind; it is rising more. A sore night for them that are out in the heather.

[MORAG *puts peat on the fire without speaking.*

MARY STEWART. Did you notice were there many people going by to-day?

MORAG. No. After daybreak the redcoats came by from Struan; and there was no more till nine, when an old man like the Catechist from Killichonan passed. At four o'clock, just when the dark was falling, a horseman with a lad holding to the stirrup, and running fast, went by towards Rannoch.

MARY STEWART. But no more redcoats?

MORAG [*shaking her head*]. The road has been as quiet as the hills, and they as quiet as the grave. Do you think will he come?

MARY STEWART. Is it you think I have the gift, girl, that you ask me that? All I know is that it is five days since he was here for meat and drink for himself and for the others—five days and five nights, mind you; and little enough he took away; and those in hiding no' used to such sore lying, I'll be thinking. He must try to get through to-night. But that quietness, with no one to be seen from daylight till dark, I do not like it, Morag. They must know something. They must be watching.

[*A sound is heard by both women. They stand listening.*

MARY STEWART. Haste you with the light, Morag.

MORAG. But it came from the back of the house—from the hillside.

MARY STEWART. Do as I tell you. The other side may be watched.

[*A candle is lit and placed in the window. Girl goes hurrying to the door.*

MARY STEWART. Stop, stop! Would you be opening the door with a light like that shining from the house? A man would be seen against it in the doorway for a mile. And who knows what eyes may be watching? Put out the light now and cover the fire.

[*Room is reduced to semi-darkness, and the door unbarred. Some one enters.*

MORAG. You are cold, Dugald!

[STEWART, *very exhausted, signs assent.*

MORAG. And wet, oh, wet through and through!

STEWART. Erricht Brig was guarded, well guarded. I had to win across the water.

[*The old woman has now relit candle and taken away plaid from fire.*

MARY STEWART. Erricht Brig—then——

STEWART [*nods*]. Yes—in a corrie, on the far side of Dearig, half-way up.

MARY STEWART. Himself is there then?

STEWART. Aye, and Keppoch as well, and another and a greater is with them.

MARY STEWART. Wheest! [*Glances at* MORAG.]

STEWART. Mother, is it that you can . . . ?

MARY STEWART. Yes, yes, Morag will bring out the food for ye to carry back. It is under the hay in the barn, well hid. Morag will bring it—— Go, Morag, and bring it.

[MORAG *enters other room or barn which opens on right.*

STEWART. Mother, I wonder at ye; Morag would never tell—never.

MARY STEWART. Morag is only a lass yet. She has never been tried. And who knows what she might be made to tell?

STEWART. Well, well, it is no matter, for I was telling you where I left them, but not where I am to *find* them.

MARY STEWART. They are not where you said now?

STEWART. No; they left the corrie last night, and I am to find them (*whispers*) in a quiet part on Rannoch moor.

MARY STEWART. It is as well for a young lass not to be knowing. Do not tell her.

[*He sits down at table, the old woman ministers to his wants.*

STEWART. A fire is a merry thing on a night like this; and a roof over the head is a great comfort.

MARY STEWART. Ye'll no' can stop the night?

STEWART. No. I must be many a mile from here before the day breaks on Ben Dearig.

MORAG *re-enters*

MORAG. It was hard to get through, Dugald?

STEWART. You may say that. I came down Erricht for three miles, and then when I reached low country I had to take to walking in the burns because of the snow that shows a man's steps and tells who he is to them that can read; and there's plenty can do that abroad, God knows.

MORAG. But none spied ye?

STEWART. Who can tell? Before dark came, from far up

on the slopes of Dearig I saw soldiers about; and away towards the Rannoch Moor they were scattered all over the country like black flies on a white sheet. A wild cat or anything that couldna fly could never have got through. And men at every brig and ford and pass! I had to strike away up across the slopes again; and even so as I turned round the bend beyond Kilrain I ran straight into a sentry sheltering behind a great rock. But after that it was easy going.

MORAG. How could that be?

STEWART. Well you see I took the boots off him, and then I had no need to mind who might see my steps in the snow.

MORAG. You took the boots off him!

STEWART [*laughing*]. I did that same. Does that puzzle your bonny head? How does a lad take the boots off a redcoat? Find out the answer, my lass, while I will be finishing my meat.

MORAG. Maybe he was asleep?

STEWART. Asleep! Asleep! Well, well, he sleeps sound enough now, with the ten toes of him pointed to the sky.

[*The old woman has taken up dirk from table. She puts it down again.* MORAG *sees the action and pushes dirk away so that it rolls off the table and drops to the floor. She hides her face in her hands.*

MARY STEWART. Morag, bring in the kebbuck o' cheese. Now that all is well and safe it is we that will look after his comfort to-night. [MORAG *goes into barn.*] . . . I mind well her mother saying to me—it was one day in the black winter that she died, when the frost took the land in its grip and the birds fell stiff from the trees, and the deer came down and put their noses to the door—I mind well her saying just before she died——

[*Loud knocking at the door.*

A VOICE. In the King's name! [*Both rise.*
MARY STEWART. The hay in the barn, quick, my son.
[*Knocking continues.*
A VOICE. Open in the King's name!

[STEWART *snatches up such articles as would reveal his presence and hurries into barn. He overlooks dirk on floor. The old woman goes towards door.*

MARY STEWART. Who is there? What do you want?
A VOICE. Open, open.

[MARY STEWART *opens door and* CAMPBELL OF KILMHOR *follows* CAPTAIN SANDEMAN *into the house. Behind* KILMHOR *comes a man carrying a leather wallet,* JAMES MACKENZIE, *his clerk. The rear is brought up by soldiers carrying arms.*

SANDEMAN. Ha, the bird has flown.
CAMPBELL [*who has struck dirk with his foot and picked it up*]. But the nest is warm; look at this.
SANDEMAN. It seems as if we had disturbed him at supper. Search the house, men.
MARY STEWART. I'm just a lonely old woman. You have been misguided. I was getting through my supper.
CAMPBELL [*holding up dirk*]. And this was your toothpick, eh? Na! na! We ken whaur we are, and wha we want, and by Cruachan I think we've got him.

[*Sounds are heard from barn, and soldiers return with* MORAG. *She has stayed in hiding from fear, and she still holds the cheese in her hands.*

SANDEMAN. What have we here!
CAMPBELL. A lass!
MARY STEWART. It's just my dead brother's daughter. She was getting me the cheese, as you can see.
CAMPBELL. On, men, again: the other turtle doo will no' be far away. [*Banteringly to the old woman*] Tut, tut,

CAMPBELL OF KILMHOR

Mistress Stewart, and do ye have her wait upon ye while your leddyship dines alane! A grand way to treat your dead brother's daughter; fie, fie upon ye!

[*Soldiers reappear with* STEWART, *whose arms are pinioned.*

CAMPBELL. Did I no' tell ye! And this, Mrs Stewart, will be your dead sister's son, I'm thinking; or aiblins your leddyship's butler! Weel, woman, I'll tell ye this: Pharaoh spared ae butler, but Erchie Campbell will no' spare anither. Na! na! Pharaoh's case is no' to be taken as forming ony preceedent. And so if he doesna answer certain questions we have to speir at him, before morning he'll hang as high as Haman.

[STEWART *is placed before the table at which* CAMPBELL *has seated himself. Two soldiers guard* STEWART. *Another is behind* CAMPBELL's *chair, and another is by the door. The clerk,* MACKENZIE, *is seated at up corner of table.* SANDEMAN *stands by the fire.*

CAMPBELL [*to* STEWART]. Weel, sir, it is within the cognizance of the law that you have knowledge and information of the place of harbour and concealment used by certain persons who are in a state of proscription. Furthermore, it is known that four days ago certain other proscribed persons did join with these, and that they are banded together in an endeavour to secure the escape from these dominions of his Majesty, King George, of certain persons who by their crimes and treasons lie open to the capital charge. What say ye? [STEWART *makes no reply.*

CAMPBELL. Ye admit this then? [STEWART *as before.*

CAMPBELL. Come, come, my lad. Ye stand in great jeopardy. Great affairs of State lie behind this which are beyond your simple understanding. Speak up and it will be the better for ye. [STEWART *silent as before.*

CAMPBELL. Look you. I'll be frank with you. No harm will befall you this night (and I wish all in this house to note my words)—no harm will befall you this night if you supply the information required. [STEWART *as before*.

CAMPBELL [*with sudden passion*]. Sandeman, put your sword to the carcase o' this muckle ass and see will it louse his tongue.

STEWART. It may be as well then, Mr Campbell, that I should say a word to save your breath. It is this: Till you talk Rannoch Loch to the top of Schiehallion ye'll no' talk me into a yea or nay.

CAMPBELL [*quietly*]. Say ye so? Noo, I widna be so very sure if I were you. I've had a lairge experience o' life, and speaking out of it I would say that only fools and the dead never change their minds.

STEWART [*quietly too*]. Then you'll be adding to your experience to-night, Mr Campbell, and you'll have something to put on to the other side of it.

CAMPBELL [*tapping his snuff-box*]. Very possibly, young sir, but what I would present for your consideration is this: While ye may be prepared to keep your mouth shut under the condition of a fool, are ye equally prepared to do so in the condition of a dead man?

[CAMPBELL *waits expectantly*. STEWART *silent as before*.

CAMPBELL. Tut, tut, now if it's afraid ye are, my lad, with my hand on my heart and on my word as a gentleman . . .

STEWART. Afraid!

[*He spits in contempt towards* CAMPBELL.

CAMPBELL [*enraged*]. Ye damned stubborn Hieland stot. . . . [*To* SANDEMAN] Have him taken out. We'll get it another way.

[CAMPBELL *rises*. STEWART *is moved into barn by soldiers*.

CAMPBELL OF KILMHOR

CAMPBELL [*walking*]. Some puling eediots, Sandeman, would applaud this contumacy and call it constancy. Constancy! Now, I've had a lairge experience o' life, and I never saw yet a sensible man insensible to the touch of yellow metal. If there may be such a man it is demonstrable that he is no sensible man. Fideelity! quotha, it's sheer obstinacy. They just see that ye want something oot o' them, and they're so damned selfish and thrawn they winna pairt. And with the natural inabeelity o' their brains to hold mair than one idea at a time they canna see that in return you could put something into their palms far more profitable. [*Sits again at table.*] Aweel, bring Mistress Stewart up.

[*Old woman is placed before him where son had been.*

CAMPBELL [*more ingratiatingly*]. Weel noo, Mistress Stewart, good woman, this is a sair predeecament for ye to be in. I would jist counsel ye to be candid. Doubtless yer mind is a' in a swirl. Ye kenna what way to turn. Maybe ye are like the Psalmist and say: "I lookit this way and that, and there was no man to peety me, or to have compassion upon my fatherless children." But, see now, ye would be wrong; and, if ye tell me a' ye ken, I'll stand freends wi' ye. Put your trust in Erchie Campbell.

MARY STEWART. I trust no Campbell.

CAMPBELL. Weel, weel noo, I'm no' jist that set up wi' them myself. There's but ae Campbell that I care muckle aboot, after a'. But, good wife, it's no' the Campbells we're trying the noo; so as time presses we'll jist "*birze yont*," as they say themselves. Noo then, speak up. [MARY STEWART *is silent.*

CAMPBELL. [*beginning grimly and passing through astonishment, expostulation, and a feigned contempt for mother and pity for son to a pretence of sadness which, except at the end, makes his words come haltingly*]. Ah! ye also. I suppose ye understand, woman, how it will go wi' your son? [*To his clerk*] Here's a fine mother for ye, James! Would you believe it? She kens what would save her son—the very babe she nursed at her breast; but will she save him? Na! na! Sir, he may look after himself! A mother, a mother! Ha! ha!

[CAMPBELL *laughs.* MACKENZIE *titters foolishly.*
CAMPBELL *pauses to watch effect of his words.*

Aye, you would think, James, that she would remember the time when he was but little and afraid of all the terrors that walk in darkness, and how he looked up to her as to a tower of safety, and would run to her with outstretched hands, hiding his face from his fear, in her gown. The darkness! It is the dark night and a long journey before him now. [*He pauses again.*
You would think, James, that she would mind how she happit him from the cold of winter and sheltered him from the summer heats, and, when he began to find his footing, how she had an eye on a' the beasts of the field and on the water and the fire that were become her enemies. And to what purpose all this care?—tell me that, my man, to what good, if she is to leave him at the last to dangle from a tree at the end of a hempen rope—to see his flesh given to be meat for the fowls of the air—her son, her little son!

MARY STEWART. My son——my little son . . . Oh, but my son is guilty of no crime!

CAMPBELL. Is he no'! Weel, mistress, as ye'll no' take my word for it, maybe ye'll list to Mr Mackenzie here. What say ye, James?

MACKENZIE. He is guilty of aiding and abetting in the concealment of proscribed persons; likewise with being found in the possession of arms, contrary to statute, both very heinous crimes.

CAMPBELL. Very well said, James! Forby, between our

selves, Mrs Stewart, the young man in my opeenion is guilty of another crime [*snuffs*]—he is guilty of the heinous crime of not knowing on which side his bread is buttered. —Come now. . . .

MARY STEWART. Ye durst not lay a finger on the lad, ye durst not hang him.

MACKENZIE. And why should the gentleman not hang him if it pleesure him ?

[CAMPBELL *taps snuff-box and takes pinch*.

MARY STEWART [*with intensity*]. Campbell of Kilmhor, lay but one finger on Dugald Stewart and the weight of Ben Cruachan will be light to the weight that will be laid on your soul. I will lay the curse of the seven rings upon your life : I will call up the fires of Ephron, the blue and the green and the grey fires, for the destruction of your soul: I will curse you in your homestead and in the wife it shelters and in the children that will never bear your name. Yea and ye shall be cursed.

CAMPBELL [*startled—betrays agitation—the snuff is spilt from his trembling hand*]. Hoot toot, woman ! ye're, ye're . . . [*Angrily*] Ye auld beldame, to say such things to me ! I'll have ye first whippet and syne droont for a witch. Damn thae stubborn and supersteetious cattle ! [*To* SANDEMAN] We should have come in here before him and listened in the barn, Sandeman !

SANDEMAN. Ah, listen behind the door you mean ! Now I never thought of that !

CAMPBELL. Did ye not ! Humph ! Well, no doubt there are a good many things in the universe that yet wait for your thought upon them. What would be your objections, now ?

SANDEMAN. There are two objections, Kilmhor, that you would understand.

CAMPBELL. Name them.

SANDEMAN. Well, in the first place, we have not wings like crows to fly . . . and the footsteps on the snow . . . Second point—the woman would have told him we were there.

CAMPBELL. Not if I told her I had power to clap her in Inverness jail.

MARY STEWART [*in contempt*]. Yes, even if ye had told me ye had power to clap me in hell, Mr Campbell.

CAMPBELL. Lift me that screeching Jezebel oot o' here; Sandeman, we'll mak' a quick finish o' this. [*Soldiers take her towards barn.*] No, not there, pitch the old girzie into the snow.

MARY STEWART. Ye'll never find him, Campbell, never, never!

CAMPBELL [*enraged*]. Find him, aye, by God I'll find him, if I have to keek under every stone on the mountains from the Boar of Badenoch to the Sow of Athole. [*Old woman and soldiers go outside.*] And now, Captain Sandeman, you an' me must have a word or two. I noted your objection to listening ahint doors and so on. Now, I make a' necessary allowances for youth and the grand and magneeficent ideas commonly held, for a little while, in that period. I had them myself. But, man, gin ye had trod the floor of the Parliament Hoose in Edinburry as long as I did, wi' a pair o' thin hands at the bottom o' toom pockets, ye'd ha'e shed your fine notions, as I did. Noo, fine pernickety noansense will no' do in this business——

SANDEMAN. Sir!

CAMPBELL. Softly, softly, Captain Sandeman, and hear till what I have to say. I have noticed with regret several things in your remarks and bearing which are displeasing to me. I would say just one word in your ear; it is this: These things, Sandeman, are not conducive to advancement in his Majesty's service.

CAMPBELL OF KILMHOR

SANDEMAN. Kilmhor, I am a soldier, and if I speak out my mind you must pardon me if my words are blunt: I do not like this work, but I loathe your methods.

CAMPBELL. Mislike the methods you may, but the work ye must do! Methods are my business. Let me tell you the true position. In ae word it is no more and no less than this. You and me are baith here to carry out the proveesions of the Act for the Pacification of the Highlands. That means the cleaning up of a very big mess, Sandeman, a very big mess. Now, what is your special office in this work? I'll tell ye, man; you and your men are just beesoms in the hands of the law-officers of the Crown. In this district, I order and ye soop! [*He indicates door of barn.*] Now soop, Captain Sandeman.

SANDEMAN [*in some agitation*]. What is your purpose? What are you after? I would give something to see into your mind.

CAMPBELL. Ne'er fash aboot my mind: what has a soldier to do with ony mental operations? It's his Grace's orders that concern you. Oot wi' your man and set him up against the wa'.

SANDEMAN. Kilmhor, it is murder—murder, Kilmhor!

CAMPBELL. Hoots awa', man, it's a thing o' nae special signeeficance.

SANDEMAN. I must ask you for a warrant.

CAMPBELL. Quick then: Mackenzie will bring it out to you.
[*Clerk begins writing.* SANDEMAN *and soldiers lead* STEWART *outside.* CAMPBELL *sits till they are out. Clerk finishes.*

MACKENZIE. At this place, Sir.

CAMPBELL. Hoots! I was forgetting.

MACKENZIE. It is a great power ye have in your hands, Kilmhor, to be able to send a man to death on the nod, as ye might say.

CAMPBELL. Power! Power, say ye? Man, do ye no' see I'm beaten? Do ye no' see that? Archibald Campbell and a' his money and men are less to them than the wind blowing in their faces.

MACKENZIE. Well, it is a strange thing that!

CAMPBELL [*gets up*]. Aye, it is a strange thing that. It is a thing I do not understand. It is a thing fit to sicken a man o' the notion that there are probabeelities on this earth. . . . Beforehand I would have said that naething could be easier, and yet—and yet—there it is! . . . [*Paces forward.*] Man, it would have been a grand stroke for me. . . . Cluny—Keppoch—Lochiel, and maybe . . . maybe . . . Hell! when I think o' it! Heard you what he said, James? "You'll be adding to your experience to-night, Mr Campbell, and have something to put to the other side of it," says he. Aye! and I have added something to it, and by God it is a thing I like but little—that a dream can be stronger than a strong man armed. . . . Just a whispered word, a pointed finger, would ha' tell'd us a'. [*Returns to table and sits.*] But no! I am powerless before the vision of an old woman, the dream of a half-grown lad.

MACKENZIE. No' exactly powerless, Kilmhor, for if ye canna open his mouth ye can shut it, and there's aye a satisfaction in that. [CAMPBELL *signs.*]

CAMPBELL. No' to me, man, no' to me, for I've been beaten. [*Hands paper to* MACKENZIE, *who goes out.*] The pair o' them have beat me—though it's a matter of seconds till one of them be dead.

MORAG [*starts into upright position and staring at him: her voice is like an echo to his*]. Dead!

CAMPBELL [*turning hastily*]. What is that!

MORAG. Is he dead?

CAMPBELL [*grimly*]. Not yet, but if ye'll look through

CAMPBELL OF KILMHOR

this window [*he indicates window*] presently, ye'll see him gotten ready for death.

[*He begins to collect articles of personal property, hat, etc.*

MORAG. I will tell you.

CAMPBELL [*astounded*]. What!

MORAG. I will tell you all you are seeking to know.

CAMPBELL [*quietly*]. Good God, and to think, to think I was on the very act . . . in the very act of . . . tell me—tell me at once.

MORAG. You will promise that he will not be hanged?

CAMPBELL. He will not. I swear it.

MORAG. You will give him back to me?

CAMPBELL. I will give him back unhung.

MORAG. Then [CAMPBELL *comes near*], in a corrie half-way up the far side of Dearig—God save me!

CAMPBELL. Dished after a'. I've clean dished them! Loard, Loard! once more I can believe in the rationality of Thy world. [*Gathers up again his cloak, hat, etc.*] And to think . . . to think . . . I was on the very act of going away like a beaten dog!

MORAG. He is safe from hanging now?

CAMPBELL [*chuckles and looks out at window before replying, and is at door when he speaks*]. Very near it, very near it. Listen!

[*He holds up his hand—a volley of musketry is heard.* KILMHOR *goes out, closing the door behind him. After a short interval of silence, the old woman enters and advances a few steps.*

MARY STEWART. Did you hear, Morag Cameron, did you hear? [*The girl is sobbing, her head on her arms.*

MARY STEWART. Och! be quiet now, I would be listening till the last sound of it passes into the great hills and over all the wide world. . . . It is fitting for you to be crying, a child that cannot understand, but water shall never wet eye of mine for Dugald Stewart. Last night I was but the mother of a lad that herded sheep on the Athole hills: this morn it is I that am the mother of a man who is among the great ones of the earth. All over the land they will be telling of Dugald Stewart. Mothers will teach their children to be men by him. High will his name be with the teller of fine tales. . . . The great men came, they came in their pride, terrible like the storm they were, and cunning with words of guile were they. Death was with them. . . . He was but a lad, a young lad, with great length of days before him, and the grandeur of the world. But he put it all from him. "Speak," said they, "speak, and life and great riches will be for yourself." But he said no word at all! Loud was the swelling of their wrath! Let the heart of you rejoice, Morag Cameron, for the snow is red with his blood. There are things greater than death. Let them that are children shed the tears. . . .

[*She comes forward and lays her hand on the girl's shoulder.*

MARY STEWART. Let us go and lift him into the house, and not be leaving him lie out there alone.

CURTAIN

Applications regarding performances of this play should be addressed to Messrs Samuel French, Ltd., 26 Southampton Street, Strand, London, W.C.2, or 28–30 West 38th Street, New York.

THE GRAND CHAM'S DIAMOND
A PLAY IN ONE ACT
By Allan Monkhouse

Mr Allan Monkhouse, whose name is well known to all readers of *The Manchester Guardian*, is a critic, an essayist, and a novelist; but it is as a writer of plays that he has done his most notable work. He excels in delicate light comedy, and he has the rare gift of compelling people to 'think out' new ideas. His best works are "The Education of Mr Surrage" and "Mary Broome," and his latest published play is a war-study entitled "The Conquering Hero." He has also published a number of tragedies.

CHARACTERS

Mrs Perkins
Mr Perkins
Miss Perkins
A Man in Black
Albert Watkins

This play was first produced at the Birmingham Repertory Theatre on September 21, 1918, by Mr John Drinkwater, with the following cast:

Mrs Perkins . . . Cathleen Orford
Mr Perkins . . . Reginald Gatty
Miss Perkins . . . Sidney Leon
A Man in Black . . Noel Shammon
Albert Watkins . . J. Adrian Byrne

THE GRAND CHAM'S DIAMOND

SCENE: *A sitting-room in a small house in a London suburb. The window is in the wall to the left of the spectator and the door in the right half of the back wall. The furniture is ordinary. On the chimneypiece, to the right of the spectator, is a clock. The room is lit by electric light. It is some time after the evening meal.* MR PERKINS *is reading a newspaper.* MRS PERKINS *is darning a sock, and* MISS PERKINS *is engaged upon a jigsaw puzzle.*

MRS PERKINS. What I mean t' say is that it's not much fun for us.

MR PERKINS. All right, Ma.

MISS PERKINS [*engaged on her puzzle*]. Bother!

MRS P. It makes a long evenin' of it. Same every night. We 'ave our tea and then we just set down till it's time to go to bed. It's not fair.

MR P. Same for all of us.

MRS P. That it's not.

MR P. Why isn't it?

MRS P. Do y' or do y' not go out o' this 'ouse every mornin' and spend the day out?

MR P. It'd be a poor job for you if I didn't.

MRS P. I don't say anythin' about that. I don't interfere.

MR P. 'Ow could y' interfere?

MISS P. Bother!

MRS P. Don't interrup' like that when me and your pa's talkin', Polly.

MISS P. My name isn't Polly.

MR P. What is it?

MISS P. It's Marie.

MR P. Well, I'm blowed!

MRS P. An' why shouldn't she 'ave a bit of a change? She's tired of bein' Polly.

MISS P. I do think we might have a little more change.

MR P. Don't you start.

MISS P. We might have gone out to the pictures to-night, as Mother said.

MR P. Your young man might 'ave come and found you out.

MISS P. You know he's engaged in the evenings.

MR P. Yes, and what at?

MISS P. Never mind!

MRS P. I do think, Polly, that he ought to be a bit more open with you. What *does* he do?

MR P. Ay; what does Albert Watkins do?

MISS P. Never you mind!

MRS P. 'E's never told 'er.

MR P. I 'ope it's nothin' to be ashamed of.

MISS P. P'raps I know more than you think.

MRS P. 'As 'e said?

MISS P. It's confidential.

MR P. Oh! I know that tale.

MRS P. Well, Polly's got 'er young man and you've got your business an' out all day seein' people. What 'ave I got?

MR P. Well, what should y' 'ave? What does any woman 'ave? I dunno what you're botherin' about. Y' 'ad a week at Margate this year.

MRS P. [*derisively*]. 'Ome from 'ome!

MR P. A good woman ought to like 'er 'ome.

MRS P. I never said I didn't like it.

THE GRAND CHAM'S DIAMOND

MR P. Well——

MRS P. 'Ome's a place to come back to.

MISS P. Mother's romantic. That's what she is.

MRS P. What *is* that, Polly? It's a word I never rightly——

MR P. Romantic! At 'er age!

MRS P. You know what it is, do y'?

MR P. It's penny dreadfuls and the pictures and gassin' about love and the deep blue sea.

MRS P. Well, y' might do worse.

MR P. Whatever's come over 'er?

MRS P. I've always thought I should like to travel.

MISS P. [*at her puzzle*]. I think there's a bit missing.

MRS P. Eh? A bit missin'? That's the way with me; there's always bin a bit missin'.

MR P. I dunno why y're startin' like this now. Y've ad all these years to settle down in. What's come over yer?

MRS P. Eh! Don't ask me. I think 'er Albert's comin' about 'as unsettled me.

MISS P. Albert!

MRS P. Well, I see 'im an' you and I think what might 'a' been.

MR P. What's that?

MRS P. Well, I was young onct.

MR P. But y're not now.

MRS P. You've no call to throw it in m' teeth.

MR P. Teeth indeed!

MRS P. Don't be insultin', Mr Perkins.

MR P. I wasn't bein'.

MRS P. Yes, y' was.

MISS P. I don't see why Albert should unsettle you.

MRS P. If I was you I'd want to know 'ow 'e spends 'is evenings.

MISS P. It's no business of yours, Ma.

MR P. It'll be some bus'ness of mine. I think it's about time Albert spoke to me.

MISS P. Spoke to you?

MR P. Placed 'is position an' prospects before me.

MISS P. Well, I believe he's a confidential agent.

MRS P. A what!

MR P. What sort of a' agent?

MISS P. It's confidential—or financial p'raps.

MR P. He's kiddin' yer.

MRS P. Do they work at night?

MISS P. I've always understood that Rothschilds and people like that did this business at parties—on the quiet.

MR P. Bosh!

MISS P. Oh, very well, Pa.

[MISS P. *settles to her puzzle.* MRS P. *darns stolidly.* MR P. *returns to the paper. A short pause.*

MRS P. Well, it's too late for the movies now.

MISS P. Ah! That's it. [*She finds the missing bit.*]

MRS P. What's in the paper, Pa?

MR P. There's a Cabinet crisis.

MRS P. Isn't there anythin' interestin'?

MR P. 'Ere's a child stole a shillin' an' swallowed it t' escape detection.

MRS P. Poor thing!

MR P. 'Ere! Is this more in your line? Great Jewel Robbery! The Grand Cham's Diamond missing.

MRS P. Eh! What's that?

MISS P. Who is the Grand Cham?

MR P. 'E's—one o' them Eastern potentates. 'E's been stayin' at the Majestic Hotel. The dimond was taken out of the settin' and a walnut substituted.

MRS P. A walnut! It must be a whopper.

MISS P. Why did they substitute a walnut?

THE GRAND CHAM'S DIAMOND

MR P. You must substitute somethin'.

MISS P. Why?

MR P. I don't know. They always do. The brightest treasure of the East. Not the slightest trace. Supposed Asiatic gang. Sherlock Holmes and Father Brown have been summoned and a telegram despatched to Mossier Lecock.

MRS P. [*with satisfaction*]. Well, that's somethin' like.

MISS P. What's it worth?

MR P. Eh! I dunno. Thousands, thousands. They say it makes the Koh-i-noor take a back seat.

MRS P. Reelly?

MR P. What 'ud you do, old lady, if I brought it 'ome for y're birthday?

MRS P. Well, I'd wear it, I s'pose.

MISS P. You'd never dare, Ma.

MRS P. I would that.

MISS P. But thieves'd always be after it.

MRS P. What d' these thieves do with it when they've got it?

MR P. I s'pose they chop it up and sell it in bits.

MRS P. What a shame!

MR P. I dessay they're off to South America.

MRS P. Why?

MR P. No extrydition.

MRS P. What's that? D' y' mean last 'dition extra?

MISS P. No, Ma. It means that thieves can't be turned out.

MRS P. Why not?

MR P. It's like it used to be with slaves here. Once the South American flag's waved over 'em, they're all right.

MISS P. It isn't all one country there, Pa.

MR P. Well, I reckon they're much of a muchness.

MRS P. An' could you sell it there?

MR P. Yes, they're great people for jewl'ry.

MRS P. Polly, you're doin' nothin'. Y' might as well be mendin' that blind.

MISS P. Oh, bother!

MRS P. It looks bad hangin' down like that.

MISS P. [*going towards the window*]. People'll see in.

MRS P. There's not many passin' at this time o' night.

MISS P. It makes it so public. [*She takes the blind from the lower part of the window and begins to mend it.*] Where's the white thread, Ma?

MRS P. Here y' are. Now, make a job of it.

> [MR PERKINS *has returned to his paper, his daughter is more or less intent on her work,* MRS PERKINS *darns and yawns.* MR PERKINS *snores gently.*

MRS P. Might as well all be asleep.

MISS P. Listen, Ma!

MRS P. Somebody runnin'. Seem in an 'urry.

> [*Something crashes through the window and falls with broken glass upon the floor.*

MISS P. Good gracious!

MRS P. Mercy on us!

MR P. [*waking up*]. Fire! Where is it?

MRS P. Nonsense, Pa! It's them boys. Out arter 'em.

MR P. What! Where?

MISS P. No. Don't go. Don't leave us. It can't be boys.

MR P. [*seeing the broken window*]. This is very careless, Polly.

MISS P. It wasn't me. It's a stone, I think.

MRS P. They're far enough now. Where is it?

MISS P. I'm all of a tremble.

MRS P. You ought to 'ave run right out, Pa, and you might 'ave caught 'em. I never did see such a thing.

MR P. It's an outrage, this is. Did y' see anybody?

THE GRAND CHAM'S DIAMOND

MRS P. We 'eard somebody runnin'.

MISS P. I thought I 'eard somebody passing after that. Quietly like. Runnin' very light.

MR P. Nonsense, Polly. Better put that blind up now.

MISS P. You put it up.

MR P. Do as I tell you.

MISS P. I don't like.

MRS P. 'Ere, 'ere. Give it me.

[*She puts it up and peers out into the street.*

MISS P. Come away, Ma.

MR P. Where's the stone?

[*They all look about the floor.*

MISS P. Here it is. Here's something. [*She picks it up.*] Why! it's a lump of glass.

MR P. Let's look!

MRS P. Let me see. [*They crowd round.*

MR P. I say!

MISS P. What is it? What is it?

MRS P. Give it me, Polly. [*She grabs it.*]

MR P. Hold it up to the light.

MISS P. Why! What can it be?

MRS P. [*relinquishing it to her husband*]. Nonsense! Nonsense!

[*She goes back to her chair and begins to fumble with her darning. She is greatly agitated.*

MR P. It's a rum thing, this is.

MISS P. Eh! Isn't it beautiful?

MR P. It might be a——

MISS P. Diamond?

MR P. Nonsense!

MRS P. [*rushing forward*]. Hide it!

[*She seizes the diamond and looks about the room.*

MISS P. Why! What d' y' mean, Ma?

MRS P. It's it.

183

MR P. [*feebly*]. What's it?
MRS P. You know.
MR P. What—what—what rubbish! The idea!
MRS P. [*looking at it in her palm*]. It's the Grand Cham's dimond.
MR P. Then it's dangerous.
MRS P. Never mind that.
MISS P. What shall we do? [*She begins to whimper.*]
MRS P. Stop that, Polly.
MR P. P'raps we'd better look out for a policeman.
MRS P. No.
MR P. If it is it we're not safe.
MRS P. I don't care.
MR P. But what d' y' want to do?
MRS P. Here! Let's put it inside the clock. [*She opens the back of the clock and crams it in.*] Now!
MR P. What are y' up to, Ma?
MISS P. I wish you'd throw it out in the street again.
MRS P. No, no.
MR P. But what *are* y' up to?
MRS P. It's come to us, this 'as. We'll stick to it if we can.
MR P. But——
MISS P. Oh, Ma!
MRS P. They may not find the 'ouse again. They're all alike in this street.
MR P. There's the broken window.
MRS P. Let's 'ave the bits of glass out. Then it won't be noticed.

> [*She peers out into the street. Then she begins to pluck the fragments of broken glass from the window. She winces and licks her finger.*

MR P. You've cut yourself now.
MRS P. Never mind that. Polly, pick all the bits off the

THE GRAND CHAM'S DIAMOND

floor. Don't leave a trace. [*She licks her finger.* POLLY *obeys.*]

MR P. Now, what's all this about?

MISS P. [*on the floor*]. I dunno what's come over 'er.

MRS P. 'Ere, Polly, look alive. 'Ave y' got 'em all?

MISS P. All I can find.

MRS P. Drat it! A bit's fallen outside. Go out and pick it up, Pa. No; p'raps better not.

MR P. Look here! What's y're game?

MRS P. Give here! [*She takes all the fragments together and puts them under the sofa cushion. She looks round the room, listens at the window and returns to her darning.*] If anyone comes, mind we know nothin' about it.

MR P. It depends 'oo comes, doesn't it?

MRS P. No.

MR P. It might be the police.

MRS P. Never mind the police.

MR P. Why! What d' y' mean? What *do* y' mean?

MRS P. It's the chanct of a lifetime. We'll take it.

MISS P. Oh, Ma!

MR P. Look 'ere——

MRS P. It's come to us. It might a' bin the answer to a prayer.

MR P. Was it?

MRS P. Not exactly, but I've been thinkin' a lot.

MR P. More likely the devil.

MRS P. There's no such thing. Y'r talkin' nonsense.

MR P. No devil. Then is there God?

MRS P. There may be. 'E may 'av sent it.

MR P. It's awful talk, this.

MISS P. Why! What could you do with it?

MRS P. Chop it up and sell it.

MR P. Where?

MRS P. In South America.

MR P. Good 'eavens!

MISS P. Ma, how can you?

MR P. 'Ave y' took leave of y'r senses?

MRS P. Yes, if y' like.

MR P. Well, I've 'eard tell as women aren't honest like men and now I know it.

MRS P. 'Ow do I know you're honest?

MR P. I've never a took a thing in my life. I've a record, 'aven't I?

MRS P. I dessay. I dunno. I won't give it up. I won't. I won't. So there!

MR P. 'Ow can y' 'elp it?

MRS P. I've sat there darnin' and mendin', waitin' and dozin' till I'm tired. I've never 'ad a go at anythin'. The chanct 'as come.

MISS P. I did think you were honest, Ma.

MRS P. Honest! It's ours.

MR P. 'Ow can it be?

MRS P. 'Oo's is it?

MR P. Why! That Grand Cham's.

MRS P. An' 'ow did 'e get it? 'E's a tyrant. 'E stole it off some nigger. Now it's come to me. It's mine. It's mine as much as anyone's. It's come like a miracle.

MISS P. But you can't keep it.

MR P. Y'r ma amazes me.

MRS P. First thing in the mornin' y'll get a list o' them ships sailin' for South America.

MISS P. Oh, Ma! Ma!

MR P. She's off 'er chump.

MRS P. I'll go alone if y' like.

MR P. It's dangerous. It's dangerous. There may be a revolver levelled at y' now.

MRS P. I don't care.

MR P. I never knew she was like this.

THE GRAND CHAM'S DIAMOND

MISS P. South America? Where?

MRS P. Y' shall 'ave jewels and dresses no end, Polly.

MISS P. Don't, Ma.

MR P. South America! Like that chap Jabez Balfour.

MISS P. He was brought back, wasn't he?

MR P. I object to be put along of 'im, any'ow.

MRS P. We'd manage better than that. Riches! Livin' at ease. Motors an' champagne. We've never 'ad a chanct!

MR P. It can't be done. It's all nonsense. An' it's 'orrible to think of.

MRS P. Oh! It's a beautiful thing. I couldn't bear to break it up. We'll keep it. We'll look at it now and then. Every Sunday.

MR P. Sunday!

MRS P. I could go on settin' 'ere if I knew it was there all the time. I think I could be 'appy.

MISS P. You'd never be safe.

MRS P. Safe! I've bin too safe.

MR P. Oh, missis! Oh, missis!

MISS P. It's strange nobody's come.

MRS P. Nobody's comin'. It's a gift.

MR P. It may not be—what y' think.

MRS P. [*fiercely*]. It is.

MR P. Then they'll be after us. Police—or worse.

MRS P. Let 'em come.

[*There is a ring at the door bell. They all stand tense.*]

MR P. Now, there.

MISS P. Oh, dear!

MRS P. You'll not say a word. You'll do as I tell you. Mind that. We know nothing.

MISS P. There's the window.

MRS P. Leave that to me.

MR P. Oh! But, I say——

MRS P. Thomas Perkins, you'll rue it to your dyin' day if—— [*The ring again.*

MR P. Who's goin'?

MRS P. I am. Remember! [*She goes out.*

MISS P. What are we to do, Pa?

MR P. Eh! I'm beat.

MISS P. Shall we throw it out of the window?

MR P. No, no. Best not. Humour her a bit. It may be nothin'.

MRS P. [*outside*]. No, you don't. 'Ere. I tell yer——

STRANGER. Excuse me.

MRS P. Pa, 'ere's a man forcin' 'is way——

MISS P. Oh, dear!

MR P. Dash it all! I say!

[MRS P. *and a dark* STRANGER, *dressed in black, enter together. She is resisting his advance, but he presses on ruthlessly. As he enters she gives way and changes her tactics.*

MRS P. Well, I must say! Pushin' a lady about like that! What bis'ness 'ave y' 'ere?

STRANGER. I've told you, madam.

MRS P. A fine tale! Y'r boy an' 'is glass marble! Where is 'e? I tell yer we know nothin' about it. Do we, Pa? [*Behind the* STRANGER, *with a terrific frown, she shakes her fist at him.*]

MR P. [*feebly blustering*]. Now what's all this?

MISS P. Oh, Ma!

MRS P. Shut up!

STRANGER. I'm sorry to intrude, sir, but I've lost something in your room.

MRS P. What nonsense! 'Ow could yer?

STRANGER. As I have told this lady, my little boy——

MRS P. Where is 'e?

THE GRAND CHAM'S DIAMOND

STRANGER [*to* MR P.]. His favourite glass marble. He pretended to throw it. It slipped from his hand and, I am sorry to say, went through your window. I apologize and shall be glad to pay. Please give me the—marble at once. Where is it? I've no time to lose.

MRS P. Where's the boy?

STRANGER. He's just round the corner.

MRS P. D' y' expect us to believe that tale?

STRANGER [*with a flash of menace*]. You'd better. [*To* MR P.] Now, sir!

MR P. It's a bit thick, y' know; I mean thin.

STRANGER. It will have to do. No trifling. Come!

> [*He is looking about the room, having cursorily glanced at the floor. He strides to the window and pulls down the blind.*

MRS P. None o' y'r liberties here. Get out!

MR P. 'Ere, y' know! [*Aside to* MRS P.] Ma, I don't like it.

STRANGER. The devil! Where's the glass?

MRS P. What glass?

STRANGER. The pane's gone. You see! I knew this was the house.

MRS P. That's easy explained.

MISS P. Oh, Ma! Tell him and——

MRS P. Of course I'll tell 'im. [*She menaces* MISS P. *surreptitiously.*] It's my daughter's new-fangled ideas of ventilation. She would 'ave it so. It's been that way a fortnight. No—let's see—to-day's Tuesday. Nigh on a month.

STRANGER. Damnation! Where is it! Where's the diamond?

MRS P. [*with a shriek of exultation*]. The diamond!

STRANGER. Yes, let me tell you then. Your lives are in danger. You've got the Grand Cham's diamond.

MR P. 'Ow did it get 'ere?

STRANGER. The thief was pursued. He threw it in.

MR P. [*querulously*]. Why did 'e throw it in 'ere?

STRANGER. Don't be a fool.

MRS P. An 'oo are you?

STRANGER. I am—the Grand Cham's representative.

MRS P. Prove it.

STRANGER. Enough of this.

[*He draws a revolver.* MISS P. *shrieks.* MR P. *recoils and edges away.* MRS P. *stands firm.*

MR P. Ma! Ma!

STRANGER [*rapping the butt of the revolver on the table*]. Where is it?

MRS P. I'll tell yer.

STRANGER. At once.

MRS P. I've swallered it.

STRANGER [*greatly discomposed*]. What!

MRS P. It went down as easy as a oyster.

STRANGER. Swallowed it! You're joking!

MRS P. No. I got the idea out of the evenin' paper. Where is it, Pa? 'Ere. " Child swallows Shillin'. Curious Case."

STRANGER. [*to the others*]. Is this true?

MISS P. Oh, I don't know.

MR P. Y' see, I was asleep.

STRANGER. Asleep!

MR P. Wasn't I, Mother?

MRS P. 'E'd sleep through anythin'.

STRANGER. D' you mean to say——? Where is it?

MRS P. I've just told yer.

STRANGER. On your oath——

MRS P. Oath! D' y' doubt the word of a lady?

STRANGER. Then—d' you feel it—I mean—whereabouts is it now?

THE GRAND CHAM'S DIAMOND

MRS P. I don't think that's a question a gentleman 'd ask.

STRANGER. Kites of hell! You'll have to be cut open.

MRS P. Nay, I won't.

STRANGER [*to himself*]. Cremation? Would it melt the diamond?

MRS P. I won't be cremated. There! Y' 've to get the deceased's consent. I'm goin' to be buried when my time comes.

STRANGER. [*pacing about in agitation while* MRS P. *controls the others by nods and winks.*] What's to be done? An emetic?

MRS P. You'd better go 'ome an' say it's lost.

STRANGER. Unhappy woman! Do you understand that your life is a trifle, a pawn in the game?

MRS P. Pawn! Yes, an' y' can't get it out without the ticket.

STRANGER. It's impossible. It can't be. [*He turns on the others.*] The truth! Did she swallow it? If she did, she dies.

MISS P. Oh, no, no. She didn't.

MRS P. You silly!

MISS P. Oh, Ma!

MR P. Ma, Ma, what can we do?

MRS P. Y' can 'old y'r tongues. Y'r no 'elp at all.

STRANGER. What folly this is! What can you do with it? That diamond means death to you. Death! Destruction! You haven't a chance of keeping it. You're mad. Your lives now are not worth a minute's purchase.

MISS P. Give it up, Ma. I'll tell you where it is. It's——

MRS P. [*in a terrible voice*]. Stop!

MR P. What can you do, Ma? Chuck it! Chuck it!

MRS P. 'E don't bluff me. 'E's in a great 'urry. I believe 'e's the thief.

STRANGER. Thousand devils! We're wasting time. [*He looks at the clock and then plucks out his watch.*] Your clock's slow. It's stopped. It was that time when I came in.

MISS P. Tell him. Tell him.

MR P. Oh, chuck it!

STRANGER [*perceiving that he is getting 'warm'*]. What stopped the clock?

MISS P. [*hysterically*]. Give it 'im.

MRS P. Polly, I'm ashamed of yer.

> [*A face appears at the window, but they do not see it.*

STRANGER. Is it there?

> [*He makes for the clock, and* MRS P. *throws herself in front.*

MRS P. No, it's not; and y' shan't meddle with my furniture.

STRANGER [*pointing the revolver at her*]. Move aside!

MRS P. Move aside yerself.

STRANGER [*he hesitates, then turns the revolver on* MISS P.]. Is it there? Quick!

> [MISS P. *shrieks, a hand with a revolver in it is thrust through the empty pane, the revolver is fired, the* STRANGER *drops his, stamps, curses, and wrings his hands. A man opens the window-sash and springs into the room.*

MISS P. Albert!

MRS P. What! It's Albert.

> [*The* STRANGER *rushes to the switch and turns off the light. Darkness, shouting, and confusion. The light is turned on. The furniture is disarranged, the* STRANGER *and the clock have gone, the others are distributed about the room,* MRS P. *sitting in the chair she first occupied.*

THE GRAND CHAM'S DIAMOND

ALBERT. Who's got it?
MR P. He's gone.
MISS P. Oh! Albert!
ALBERT. Where's the diamond?
MR P. It was in the clock.
ALBERT. The clock? Where is it?
MISS P. Oh! Albert!
MR P. 'E's taken it. 'E's got the clock.
MRS P. Nay, 'e 'asn't.
    [*She produces the clock from under her petticoats.*
MR P. Well, I'm blowed!
MISS P. Oh, Ma!
ALBERT. What is it? Have you got it?
MRS P. I've got it right enough.
    [*She carries the clock to the chimneypiece, opens it, and takes out the diamond.*
Will that gentleman come back?
ALBERT. No, he won't.
MRS P. How d' y' know?
ALBERT. I know.
MRS P. Polly, just put that blind back, will yer? I don't like bein' too public.
MISS P. Oh! I daren't.
ALBERT. Now, ma'am, give it to me.
MRS P. Eh?
ALBERT. Let's have it. Quick.
MRS P. Where d' you come in, Albert?
ALBERT. Come on. This'll be the making o' me.
MRS P. O' me too, I 'ope. But 'adn't we all better be movin'?
MISS P. Where to, Ma?
MRS P. Out at the back door. Pack a few things in a bag.
ALBERT. What are y' up to? Whad y'r mean?

MRS P. Now, Albert, there's no time to make explanations. We're all in at this, aren't we?

ALBERT. Well—in a way. But look here——

MRS P. South America's the place, isn't it? D' y' know anythin' o' the sailin's? Or 'ad we better cross to France? Better take the midnight train somewhere.

ALBERT. Has she gone dotty?

MRS P. Y'r all asleep. Come on, Polly. A few things in a bag. Now, Pa. Better put this light out p'raps. Is the front door shut? Look at the time-table, Pa.

[*She is making for the door when* ALBERT *intercepts her.*

ALBERT. Give me the diamond. I dunno what y'r talkin' about.

MRS P. Nay, I stick to this.

ALBERT. You can't! What nonsense! Give it here! This job's the making o' me. Let's have it.

MRS P. Nay, it's mine an' I'll stick to it.

ALBERT. Yours!

MRS P. Yes. Dimonds like this belongs to them as can get 'em. Nobody's honest with things like this. I got it an' y' shall all share. But it's mine. It's mine. Eh! It's a beauty. I'd stick to this if all the p'lice in London was after me.

ALBERT. Y'd do what?

MRS P. Ay, an' Scotland Yard too.

ALBERT. Bah! *I'm* Scotland Yard.

MRS P. What!

MISS P. Oh! Albert!

ALBERT. Didn't y' know? Didn't y' guess? Didn't y' understand? What did y' take me for?

MRS P. D'y mean to say ——?

ALBERT. I mean t' say it's 'igh time I was on my way back with this dimond. The gang's all rounded up by this time.

THE GRAND CHAM'S DIAMOND

MISS P. The gang?

MR P. That feller was one of 'em, then? Where is he?

ALBERT. He was copped when he left 'ere. Y' didn't know y'r 'ouse was surrounded.

MRS P. But 'ow did the dimond come 'ere? 'Oo threw it in?

ALBERT. I did.

MISS P. You!

MR P. You did!

ALBERT. I did that.

MR P. Why?

ALBERT. Becos they were after me. I was a dead man if I stuck to it then. I threw it in 'ere to gain time and knowin' the 'ouse.

MISS P. Well, I never!

ALBERT. They're a desp'rate lot.

MR P. It's all most unusual. Never since I've been an 'ouse'older 'ave I——

MISS P. Oh, Albert! You might 'ave told me.

ALBERT. I 'ad my reasons.

MRS P. Y'r a detective, then?

ALBERT. I am that. So let's 'ave it. I tell yer I must be off.

MRS P. [*holding up the diamond, but away from him*]. Look at it, Albert!

ALBERT. I see it.

MRS P. Can y' be honest? Look at it!

ALBERT. She's off 'er chump.

MR P. She doesn't reely mean it. I've borne a 'igh character all my life.

MRS P. [*passionately*]. It's *my* dimond.

MISS P. I'm ashamed of my ma.

MR P. My employers 'as always put the utmost confidence in me.

ALBERT. What's she up to? Now, ma'am, you'll just 'and that over or——

MRS P. Or?

ALBERT [*he produces a whistle*]. I wouldn't 'andle yer myself.

MRS P. That's it, is it?

ALBERT. That's it.

MRS P. Then let it go the way it came. [*She throws it through the window.*]

MR P. 'Old on. There's another pane gone!

ALBERT. O 'ell! [*He rushes out.*]

MISS P. You'll ruin us, Ma.

MRS P. [*dusting one hand against the other*]. A good shuttance.

MISS P. [*at the window*]. Oh! I hope he'll find it. There he is, and a policeman's with him. They've got it, I think. Yes. Albert, Albert! I wish he'd look up. They're seeing if it's damaged. There! He's waved his hand.

MRS P. [*she has settled into her chair*]. Well, we've 'ad quite a busy evenin'.

MISS P. I don't know what Albert'll think of you.

MRS P. 'E's not going to marry me, thank 'eaven.

MR P. D' y' want t' know what *I* think of yer?

MRS P. Go on! Y've no 'magernation.

MISS P. I never thought to be ashamed of my own mother.

MR P. Wantin' in the very el'ments of morality. I wonder 'ow Sossiety 'd get on if they was all like you.

MRS P. Polly, put up that blind. It's a bit chilly with them broken panes.

MISS P. Most unladylike as well.

[*They settle down into their chairs again.* MRS P. *takes up her darning and* MR P. *the paper. After*

THE GRAND CHAM'S DIAMOND

putting up the blind MISS P. *returns to her puzzle.*

MRS P. 'Ow much did y' say it was worth, Pa?

MR P. [*gruffly*]. Never mind.

MRS P. Well, I 'ad my bit o' fun for onct.

CURTAIN

Applications regarding amateur performances of this play should be addressed to the author, Mr Allan Monkhouse, Meadow Bank, Disley, Cheshire, or to Mr Le Roy Phillips, 41 Winter Street, Boston, Massachusetts, U.S.A.

THREAD O' SCARLET
A PLAY IN ONE ACT
BY J. J. BELL

Mr J. J. Bell is one of the most versatile authors now living. He made his name with humorous studies of Scottish character like *Wee Macgregor*, *Courtin' Christina*, and many others; but it is a great mistake to imagine that Mr Bell confines himself to stories in this vein. He has written some excellent sea-stories (like *The Whalers*), and might easily have won fame as another Conrad rather than as another Jacobs. Like W. W. Jacobs, too, he has written some powerful stories, and some of the best examples of his work may be found in *Some Plain—Some Coloured*.

"Thread o' Scarlet" is a grim play, intensely dramatic, and (like Lord Dunsany's "A Night at an Inn") was written at a sitting, between ten o'clock at night and four o'clock in the morning.

CHARACTERS

MIGSWORTH
SMITH } *village tradesmen*
BUTTERS
LANDLORD OF INN
BREEN, *an odd-job man*
A TRAVELLER

THREAD O' SCARLET

SCENE: *Smoke-room of a small village inn, some eight miles from the county town. Low ceiling. Broad window with screens L. Fire R., ruddy embers. Door opening on passage at back. Barely furnished. Several small tables with their complements of chairs. Crude old-fashioned oleographs on walls. Bell-rope at side of fireplace. An evening in February, about twenty minutes from closing time. A bitter wind is blowing outside, coming in squalls, with blatters of sleet against the window.*

TIME: *The present.*

MIGSWORTH, SMITH, *and* BUTTERS *are seated at a table, tankards before them.* MIGSWORTH, *who fancies himself a bit superior intellectually, and* SMITH, *a genial, rather stupid person, are interested in what is passing at back.* BUTTERS *appears sunk in his own thoughts; he is a big, heavy man; throughout the play he has a semi-dazed look. The door is open; the* LANDLORD *is standing in the entrance as if to block it, and* BREEN *is seen in the passage beyond.*

LANDLORD [*in tone of finality*]. No, Mr Breen, I can't serve ye, and my advice to you is to go home, and to bed!

BREEN. Haven't I told ye, ye'll get the money in the mornin'?

LANDLORD. Quite so. But that's not my point. I've got a licence to lose. In other words——

BREEN. Come on, gimme a bottle o' whisky!

LANDLORD. No! Ye've had enough.

BREEN. Damn ye! [*Goes out.*
[*His footfalls are heard going down passage, steadily, and then the slam of the front door. The* LANDLORD, *wiping his brow, comes into the room.*

MIGSWORTH. Quite right, Mr Flett. He's had more'n enough.

SMITH. Queer, though, how steady he walks! Don't he, Butters?

BUTTERS [*as one awakening*]. Who? Oh, Breen! I'm sick o' Breen. Never out o' my shop spyin' around and tryin' to get somethin' for nothin'. Was there to-night when I was closin'. Had to turn him out. [*Relapses.*]

LANDLORD. 'Tis his head, not his legs, that takes it all. To tell the truth, gentlemen, I'm afraid—not of, but *for* him. Trade's rotten bad, the Lord knows, but I swear I'd sooner be without Breen's custom. He's been hard at it for a solid month, and gettin' worse every day. Can't think when or where he earns the money.—But you rang, gentlemen.

MIGSWORTH [*with a wave towards tankards*]. Same again, please. [LANDLORD *makes to collect tankards.*

BUTTERS [*as if waking*]. No more for me. Must be goin' home.

MIGSWORTH. Tut! ye need another. We all do, after what we've gone through to-day.

[BUTTERS *lets his tankard go.*
And mind ye, Mr Flett, I don't wonder at Breen goin' it hard after all *he's* gone through—lost his only friend. Both shiftless chaps, but——

LANDLORD. True, true, Mr Migsworth. Still, I prefer to see a man drownin' his sorrows in moderation. [*Goes out with tankards.*]

THREAD O' SCARLET

MIGSWORTH. Ah, what a day. Longest I've ever known.

SMITH. Not so long as last night must ha' been to Jacob Forge.

BUTTERS [*without raising his head*]. Last night—oh, my soul! [*His friends glance at him.*

SMITH. Aye, ye must ha' felt it, Butters, havin' been on the jury. Always wondered why ye didn't get out o' that. I believe ye could. [*More cheerfully*] And yet, here's the three o' us, sittin' round this table for close on three hours, chattin' about 'most everything but the thing we're thinkin' on.

MIGSWORTH. Well, as two single men and a widower without offspring [*nods at* BUTTERS], 'twouldn't be natural to sit alone in our houses, dumb, and thinkin' o' Jacob Forge, our neighbour—that was. I couldn't do it.

SMITH [*in a burst of emotion*]. Oh, oh, to think that at eight o'clock this blessed—I mean cursed—mornin' Jacob Forge was hanged by—by the neck until he was——

[BUTTERS *makes a fluttering gesture of protest.*

MIGSWORTH. 'Sh! No need for to go into details, Mr Smith. Forge has paid the penalty o' his crime, havin' been found guilty by a jury o' good men and true, includin' our friend and neighbour here, William Butters, who——

BUTTERS [*sitting up*]. I must be gettin' home. 'Tis on my mind that I left the keys o' my safe on the counter and didn't lock up anything properly. Was too upset. [*Half rises and subsides.*]

MIGSWORTH. Don't you worry, Mr Butters. Your property's all right. Aye, we may pity Jacob Forge, though none o' us liked him; but we know he had a fair trial and full justice. Not that I'd ever ha' dreamed o' him bein' a murd——

BUTTERS. Don't say it! 'Tis too awful. Jacob was a

strange man, and yet—— [*Pause.*] And, of course, we found him guilty because o' the evidence.

SMITH. Of course! Because o' the evidence! But, this mornin', when I see the black flag goin' up—they did hoist it slow!—I says to myself——

MIGSWORTH. Was *you* there?

SMITH. Aye; I saw ye, too, all muffled up. 'Twas a cold mornin', though. Was muffled up myself. And you, Mr Butters—I *thought* I saw ye, too.

BUTTERS [*bowing his head*]. I went—to pray—to pray that the black flag—might never go up. Oh, my soul!

MIGSWORTH. Now, what do ye mean by that?

[LANDLORD *enters. There is a short pause while he sets the tankards on the table.*

We're talkin' o' the melancholy episode o' this mornin', Mr Flett. [*Lays money on table.*]

LANDLORD. Ah, yes, yes. Very shockin' to be sure, very shockin'. [*Taking money*] Thank 'ee, sir. I understood from his remarks that Mr Breen had been there.

SMITH. What? Him?

MIGSWORTH. How could he?—his only friend bein' hanged!

LANDLORD. He was talkin' o' puttin' a knife in the judge that sentenced Forge—and poisonin' all the jury!

SMITH. That's awful! He must be goin' crazy.

MIGSWORTH [*sagely*]. When a man takes to Scotch, he's done!

SMITH [*with an attempt at humour*]. Beggin' your pardon —but judgin' from Mister Breen's case, I should say he's never done!

MIGSWORTH. Oh, very good, very good! [*Laughs discreetly.*]

BUTTERS [*shuddering*]. What if Breen is right?

MIGSWORTH. Right?

THREAD O' SCARLET

BUTTERS. About the judge. And what—what's to happen to the judge and jury, if we was all wrong?

LANDLORD [*puzzled*]. What's all this, Mr Butters?

[BUTTERS *relapses without response.*

MIGSWORTH [*confidentially*]. Nerves, Mr Flett, just nerves.

LANDLORD. *I* see, *I* see! And I knows a little about 'em, too. Fact is, I'm a bit that way at the moment.

SMITH. How so? [*Eager to drink, nods to* MIGSWORTH.] Good health! [*Drinks.*]

LANDLORD. I've got a notion—a preminotion, if ye understand what I mean, gentlemen—that our unfortunate friend Breen'll come back to-night; and I don't like it.

MIGSWORTH. Ye'll have our support, Mr Flett—our moral support—in refusin' him refreshment.

LANDLORD. Thank 'ee, sir, thank 'ee. I'm bound to refuse him. There's my conscience to be considered——

SMITH. *And* your licence. Besides, most likely he's got no money.

LANDLORD. True, Mr Smith. [*Goes out.*

SMITH. Come away, Butters! This is real good beer—make ye sleep sound.

BUTTERS [*as if awakening*]. I saw Breen there this mornin'. Our mufflin's was nothin' to his. But I spied his face—my God, shall I ever forget his face when the flag was goin' up and——

SMITH [*eagerly*]. What was it like?

MIGSWORTH. 'Sh! Mr Smith. Suppused with grief, no doubt!

BUTTERS. 'Twas like a—a soul in torments.

MIGSWORTH. Seems to have some decent feelin's after all, though I *have* doubted it when seein' him sittin' there [*points towards corner*] night after night, drinkin' on his own. [*Drinks.*] Shows how careful we should be in judgin' our neighbours.

SMITH [*after a long pull*]. Ah, well, maybe there was more real friendship 'twixt him and Forge than we thought. They was both such terrible close chaps.

[*Motor horn is heard.*

Hullo, goin' to stop here. [*Rises and goes to window.*] My! I don't envy any man his car on a night like this! Black as hell; sleet drivin' well-nigh level! Ugh! [*Shivers.*] Glad I haven't far to go. [*Starts back from a vivid flare of lightning, which is followed quickly by a frightful thunder-clap.*]

[BUTTERS, *with a cry, leaps and subsides trembling.*

MIGSWORTH [*with feigned coolness*]. Bit unexpected at this season, wasn't it? Why, Mr Butters, ye're lookin' sickish! No danger, ye know.

BUTTERS [*with emotion*]. Oh, there's somethin' wrong in the world this night—some awful wickedness abroad—I'm feared to take the road now——

SMITH [*returning to table*]. Come, come, this won't do at all! Take a good sup o' your beer. Give ye comfort. Ye should never ha' gone to the hangin' this mornin'.

BUTTERS [*still trembling*]. I tell ye—in yon flash I saw Jacob Forge, and he was hung—hung on a scarlet thread.

[MIGSWORTH *and* SMITH *look at each other.*

MIGSWORTH. Tut! Tut!

BUTTERS [*frantically*]. Nothin' but a scarlet thread—and he was dead and starin' and his head all sideways—sorter smilin' to himself as if——

SMITH [*in a gasp*]. Smilin'!

MIGSWORTH. Hush!

[*Door opens.* TRAVELLER *enters followed by* LANDLORD.

TRAVELLER [*impatiently as he removes dripping wraps*]. Oh, this will do. Have a bedroom fired for me, and another for my man. But first let me have a double Scotch, some

THREAD O' SCARLET

boiling water, sugar and lemon. [*Goes to fire and stands chafing his hands.*]

LANDLORD. Yes, sir. [*Goes out.*
   [*A pause, during which* MIGSWORTH *and* SMITH *glance at the* TRAVELLER *and at each other.* BUTTERS, *chin on chest, takes no notice. There has been a lull in the storm, but now comes a blast of wind with a violent blatter of hail.*'

SMITH [*starting*]. Lord, what's that?

MIGSWORTH. Only hail. The thunder's brought it down. [*Is about to address* TRAVELLER.]

BUTTERS [*dreamily*]. Hung by a scarlet thread and smilin'—smilin' the smile o' [*voice almost fails*] an innocent man——

SMITH [*under his breath*]. Oh, I say!

MIGSWORTH [*leaning over and patting* BUTTERS'S *shoulder*]. Don't you worry about it, old man. [*Winking to* SMITH] I doubt he must ha' been loadin' up before he came here. [*Clears throat and addresses* TRAVELLER.] Terrible night, sir.

TRAVELLER [*turning*]. Horrible! [*Drily yet courteously*] I hope I am not intruding here. Only place with a fire going.

MIGSWORTH. Not at all, sir. 'Tis a public room, and, if 'twas private, ye'd be welcome on such a night.

TRAVELLER. Much obliged, I'm sure. [*Takes chair at hearth. Yawns. Produces case and selects a cigarette. Lights up while* MIGSWORTH *and* SMITH *watch him with interest.*] There's a village about here, isn't there?

MIGSWORTH. Two, sir. Lower Ashley and Upper Ashley. This inn is midway betwixt them.

TRAVELLER. If you reside here, perhaps you can tell me whether the population includes a person—a man—who is stone-deaf—possibly dumb also.

MIGSWORTH. Oh, no, sir.

SMITH [*hopefully*]. But we've got a paralytic, sir.

TRAVELLER. H'm! This man was apparently bound for one of the Ashleys, and he gave my chauffeur and me the nerve-shock of our lives.

[LANDLORD *enters with tray; sets it on small table which he places conveniently for the* TRAVELLER.

MIGSWORTH [*respectfully*]. How was that, sir?

TRAVELLER [*to* LANDLORD]. Thanks. [*While he mixes toddy*] Well, in the midst of a blizzard, the lamps showed him walking in the middle of the road. We kept sounding the horn, but he paid no attention. We slowed and my man was going to risk the ditch, when the fellow stepped aside, and we carried on. Next moment he was back in the middle of the road.

[*The* LANDLORD, *who has moved to the door, halts, listening*.

It was the nearest thing! Of course we braked hard, but I swear the bonnet touched him when the car stopped with a jerk that, I thought, had finished her—and then the fellow walked on without so much as turning his head. [*Sips toddy.*]

MIGSWORTH. My gracious! did ever one hear the like o' that? What did ye do, sir?

TRAVELLER. Shouted on him to stop, but he paid no attention. I think he must have left the road soon after, for when we got going again—the car had suffered, you understand—there was no sign of him. [*Savagely*] I'd like very much to get a word with him!

MIGSWORTH. Sounds like a lunatic, sir. And ye never saw his face?

TRAVELLER. Nothing but his back. [*Sips.*] A biggish man, in a long tarpaulin coat and a soft felt hat.

SMITH. Plenty o' tarpaulins and soft felts—old ones—hereabouts.

THREAD O' SCARLET

TRAVELLER. He had a heavy muffler coming above the coat-collar as if to shield the back of his head. I noted it in the lamp-light—a scarlet muffler——

[SMITH *starts as if shot.*

MIGSWORTH [*in a screech*]. A what!!!

LANDLORD [*clutching edge of door, mutters*]. A scarlet muffler! [*Slowly* BUTTERS *comes out of a dream.*

TRAVELLER. Yes. Odd taste, no doubt, but so it was—— I say, what's the matter with your friend? [*Indicates* BUTTERS.]

MIGSWORTH. Kindly excuse him, sir; he's had rather much.

BUTTERS [*muttering*]. Hung on a scarlet thread, he was, and smilin'——

MIGSWORTH [*soothingly*]. Come, come, old man!

BUTTERS [*as though not hearing, turns slowly to* TRAVELLER *and extends shaking forefinger*]. 'Twas a ghost ye saw this night—the ghost o' Jacob Forge that was hung for murder this mornin' at Lakeford Jail. And he was hung on a thread o' that same scarlet muffler—God rest his soul! [*Relapses into dream.*]

TRAVELLER [*to* MIGSWORTH]. I'm afraid all this is beyond me. Incidentally, I should say your friend is not suffering from any over-indulgence, but from some severe mental and nervous strain.

SMITH [*anticipating* MIGSWORTH]. 'Tis like enough, sir. William Butters is a good man, and as honest as any grocer could be, in these hard times. Had his difficulties, he had. But he should never ha' gone to see the black flag hoisted this mornin'. Ye see, sir, he had the ill luck to be one o' the jury that sent Jacob Forge, our neighbour, though not our friend, to the gallows, and he's never got over it. Now he's started sayin' to himself: "What if me and the judge was wrong?"

TRAVELLER [*nodding sympathetically*]. And this Jacob Forge—and the scarlet muffler?

SMITH. Why, sir——

MIGSWORTH [*interposing*]. In the winter-time Jacob Forge always wore the scarlet muffler—he was well known by it, for there was nothin' like it in Ashley. And on a dark night, on the high road, he murdered an old farmer comin' home from market wi' a bag o' money—near four hundred pounds —beat in his head wi' a hammer, he did!

SMITH. I know that money-bag! Seen it often in my shop.

LANDLORD. Same here! Farmer Jukes never passed my door——

SMITH. And they found the hammer hid in Forge's tool-house wi' blood and a grey hair or two on it. And they found three cheques belongin' to the farmer there also; but the bag o' notes and cash they never found; he must ha' hid it too safe. And 'twas proved that he was needin' money at the time. We all was, for that matter. Of course at the trial he denied everything; said he was sleepin' in his bed when it happened.

MIGSWORTH. But it was the muffler did for him! Though there was other evidence. He must ha' hid it, too, or burned it, for 'twas never found—he swore he had lost it; thought he had dropped it in one o' the village shops, but couldn't say which——

SMITH. But in the farmer's nails they got a thread of it. The old man would be clawin' at his enemy, ye understand. So 'tis true enough that Jacob Forge was hung on a thread o' scarlet.

LANDLORD [*taking a step forward and clearing his throat*]. It should be told, sir, that, even after he was condemned, Forge always believed—or pretended he believed —that something would happen to save him. But [*shaking*

THREAD O' SCARLET

his head] the black flag went up, sure enough, this mornin'! I didn't know Forge—he never came here—but I allow it has been a sorrowful day.

[*A clock is heard striking ten.*

TRAVELLER. Bound to cast a gloom over the place. Was this Forge married?

MIGSWORTH [*getting in first*]. No, sir; and he had no friends exceptin' a chap called Breen—another solitudinarian like himself—who has unfortunately been tryin' to drown his grief ever since—as Mr Flett there will confirm.

LANDLORD. Too true, sir, though I do my best to check him. [*Takes out watch; to the three*] Well, gentlemen, I'm real sorry, but the law must be obeyed.

[MIGSWORTH *empties his tankard.*

SMITH. Your clock's fast. Considerin' the day it's been and considerin' the night it is—hark to that blast!—Mr Migsworth and me ought to have one more. We'll take it standin' if ye like. [*Empties his tankard.*]

LANDLORD [*holding up watch*]. Correct time's here, gentlemen. Sorry, very sorry, indeed!

[*They rise reluctantly.* MIGSWORTH *is about to arouse* BUTTERS.

TRAVELLER. Perhaps you gentlemen will give me your company for a little longer. [*They smile delightedly.* Right! Two pints, Landlord.

LANDLORD. Very good, sir. If ye'll excuse me, I'll lock up first. [*Goes out.*

SMITH. 'Tis too kind.

MIGSWORTH [*in his best manner*]. I am deeply obliged.

[*They sit.*

TRAVELLER. Not at all. But what about your friend?

MIGSWORTH. Best not disturb him, sir. Mr Smith and me will see him home in due season. He should never ha' been on the jury.

TRAVELLER [*lighting fresh cigarette*]. What do you two gentlemen think about your friend's ghost theory?

MIGSWORTH. Well, sir, personally, I don't believe in ghosts as a general rule——

SMITH. Nor me—ever!

MIGSWORTH. All the same, I'd swear there's not a livin' man within twenty miles o' Ashley would wear a scarlet muffler now——

SMITH. Hadn't thought o' that. [*Suddenly listening, holds up hand.*] I say, there's somebody comin' in.

[*Disturbance outside; altercation.* LANDLORD's *voice:* "*No, no, I can't have it. After ten, you know!*"]

MIGSWORTH. Oh, Lord! I do believe 'tis Breen come back.

TRAVELLER. Breen?—the friend of the murd—the dead man?

MIGSWORTH. Yes, sir; and I'm afraid it means trouble for Flett. Of course Flett *can't* serve him now.

[*Altercation sounds nearer.* BREEN *cursing;* LANDLORD *protesting or trying to soothe.*]

Oh, damn it all, he's comin' in! Hope he won't be unpleasant, sir.

LANDLORD [*outside*]. Now, now, Mr Breen, don't ye be unkind. Ye wouldn't like me to lose my licence. It's after hours and if anyone saw ye comin' in—— Oh, why didn't I lock the door on the stroke?

BREEN [*outside*]. Lemme pass! Fetch a bottle o' whisky. I've got the money. Hear that? All right, fetch it!

LANDLORD. Stop, stop, for the Lord's sake!

[*Sounds of a struggle.*]

Well, well, if I let ye in for a minute, will ye promise not to——? Oh, dear!

[BREEN *enters, flinging the door back on its hinges, followed by dismayed and dishevelled* LANDLORD.

THREAD O' SCARLET

He wears a tarpaulin coat buttoned to the chin and streaming wet. He is hatless. His face is dead white; his eyes fixed and staring. He walks in a steady, mechanical fashion to a chair in the corner, his usual place. Takes no notice of other occupants. Sits.

LANDLORD [*halting just inside door, apologetically*]. Gentlemen, I couldn't stop him.

TRAVELLER [*under his breath*]. Heavens, what a case! [*Beckons* LANDLORD.]

BREEN [*staring at vacancy; in a sing-song voice*]. A knife for the silly old judge and a bottle o' whisky for me!

[LANDLORD *comes on tiptoe.*

TRAVELLER [*whispering*]. Whatever happens, not a drop!

LANDLORD. Oh, never! [*Whispering*] But *is* he—*is* he drunk, sir?

TRAVELLER. Worse! He's on the verge of—never mind. Go back to the door. Wait. Be ready.

BREEN [*without moving*]. Poison for the daft jury, and a bottle o' whisky for me!

[*The* TRAVELLER, *gripping the arms of his chair, leans forward, alert, watchful.* SMITH *stares stupidly.* BUTTERS *seems to be coming out of his dream.*

MIGSWORTH [*with a cough, behind his hand*]. What about givin' him some strong coffee, sir?

[TRAVELLER *makes a sign for silence. All is still in the room; but outside the wind rises to a shriek, and a gust of hail strikes the window.*

BREEN [*as before*]. Bottle o' whisky——

[BUTTERS *realizes presence of* BREEN *and sits quietly, gazing. There comes a flash of lightning, a crackle of thunder. All start save* BREEN. *The wind falls with a sob. Silence.*

BREEN [*as before*]. Bottle o' whisky. [*Then his expression changes as though another idea had entered his brain.*] Money!—ye want money——! [*Like an automaton he stands up. The two lowest buttons of the tarpaulin are undone, and drawing aside the skirt he gets at a pocket. Withdraws his fist, stands rigid for a moment or two.*] Money! [*Flings handful of coins on the floor.*] Money!—Whisky!

[*No one stirs.*
Not enough money? Eh? [*Goes to pocket again. Fetches forth good-sized canvas bag.*] Bottle o' whisky! [*Flings bag with a crash at* LANDLORD's *feet.*] There!

LANDLORD [*recoiling in horror*]. Oh, my good God! The farmer's money-bag!

> [SMITH, *clutching* MIGSWORTH's *arm, points at bag.* BUTTERS, *his eyes starting, rises slowly and stands grasping chair-back. His lips move soundlessly.*

BREEN [*his gaze fixed again*]. Bottle o'—— [*Pause.*] Bottle o'—— [*Longer pause.*] Black flag—black flag—black—— [*Slowly his mouth opens and shuts like that of a gasping fish.*]

> [TRAVELLER *rises softly, signalling to* LANDLORD. *The gasping stops abruptly, the mouth remaining open.* BREEN *takes two mechanical steps forward.*
>
> [*The* TRAVELLER *slips nearer.* BREEN *rises on his toes.*

TRAVELLER [*to* LANDLORD]. Quick!

> [BREEN *pitches forward. The* TRAVELLER *and* LANDLORD *catch him.*

Here!—in my chair. Get off his coat. [*Undoes coat, throws it open, exposing scarlet muffler round neck and across chest.*] Why, it's the man I nearly——

SMITH [*in a high falsetto*]. Oh, oh, oh!—the farmer's money-bag—and the scarlet muffler, too!

> [MIGSWORTH *puts his hands to his face.*

THREAD O' SCARLET

TRAVELLER. Quiet! [*Lays his ear to* BREEN'*s heart—a pause—lifts a grave countenance.*]

[*A silence.* MIGSWORTH *uncovers his face.*

BUTTERS [*staggers forward, one hand to his head, the other pointing shakily*]. Breen, ye damned thief, ye've been burglin' my safe. [*Realizes the significance of his words and stands petrified.*]

[*First the* TRAVELLER, *then* MIGSWORTH, *then* SMITH *and* LANDLORD *recoil from him.*

CURTAIN

Applications regarding performances of this play should be addressed to Messrs James B. Pinker and Son, Talbot House, Arundel Street, Strand, London, W.C.2, or to Mr Le Roy Phillips, 41 Winter Street, Boston, Massachusetts, U.S.A.

BECKY SHARP

A PLAY ADAPTED FROM THE WATERLOO CHAPTERS OF "VANITY FAIR"

By Olive Conway

WILLIAM MAKEPEACE THACKERAY was born in 1811 and died in 1863. He was one of the finest writers of the nineteenth century, and his works include *Pendennis*, *Henry Esmond*, *The Newcomes*, *The Virginians*; but it was the publication of *Vanity Fair* in 1847–48 that brought him fame.

Thackeray's writing is characterized by a rich sense of humour and unaffected pathos; he is essentially a manly writer, and with his sharp and stinging satire he is the natural enemy of hypocrisy and meanness. There is something about his fluid style and his air of impartiality which compels one to associate him with Mr Galsworthy.

Thackeray wrote light verse, playful articles for *Punch*, and lectures on historical and literary subjects, but he made no serious attempt to become a dramatist. The Waterloo chapters of *Vanity Fair*, however, are full of dramatic possibilities, and the following play by Miss Olive Conway has caught the whole spirit of the novel without spilling a drop.

CHARACTERS

Rawdon Crawley
George Osborne
Joseph Sedley
Mrs Rawdon Crawley (Becky Sharp)
Mrs George Osborne (Amelia)

Brussels, 1815. A room in a hotel. The first scene takes place on June 16, and the second on the evening of the day of Waterloo, June 18.

Character Descriptions from Thackeray

BECKY. "Small and slight in person; pale, sandy-haired, and with eyes habitually cast down: when they looked up they were very large, odd, and attractive."

AMELIA. "Her nose was rather short than otherwise, and her cheeks a great deal too round and red for a heroine, but her face blushed with rosy health and her lips with the freshest of smiles, and she had a pair of eyes which sparkled with the brightest and honestest good-humour, except indeed when they filled with tears, and that was a great deal too often."

JOSEPH. "A very stout, puffy man, in buckskins and Hessian boots, with several immense neckcloths that rose almost to his nose, with a red-striped waistcoat and an apple-green coat with steel buttons. . . . Twelve years older than his sister Amelia. He was in the East India Company's Civil Service."

RAWDON. "A perfect and celebrated 'blood,' or dandy about town, was this young officer. . . . He is a very large young dandy. He is six feet high and speaks with a great voice, and swears a great deal. He has a dreadful reputation among the ladies."

GEORGE. "He was twenty-three. He was a little wild; how many young men are; and don't girls like a rake better than a milksop? . . . 'A goodish-looking fellow, with large black whiskers?' said Crawley. 'Enormous,' Miss Rebecca Sharp said, 'and enormously proud of them, I assure you.'"

BECKY SHARP

SCENE I: *A sitting-room in a hotel at Brussels, 2 A.M., June 16, 1815. Table, piano, chairs, settee. C. door to corridor. L. door to bedroom. Curtained window R.*
It is immediately after the Ball. Stage empty on rise of curtain.

Enter RAWDON CRAWLEY, *who turns up lamp and then looks expectantly at door.* BECKY *enters, in ball dress, with bouquet, but only just comes in and then turns back to door.*

BECKY. But come in, Captain Osborne. Do come in, Amelia, my sweetest, come in. [*She brings* AMELIA *in.*]

RAWDON [*towards door, in which* GEORGE OSBORNE *stands hesitating*]. Why not, Osborne?

AMELIA. It is so late, Captain Crawley.

[GEORGE *is pulled in by* RAWDON, *who closes door.*

BECKY. Late? On such a night as this there is no such word as late. Oh, the ball! That perfect, perfect ball! I've danced till I'm exalted.

AMELIA. Yes. You triumphed, Becky. I——

BECKY. You preferred not to dance. Had you shown inclination to dance, you would have danced as much as I.

GEORGE. Some women have to refuse partners. Others don't attract them. [*He is furious with* AMELIA.]

AMELIA. George!

GEORGE. Oh, look at her! No diamonds. No bouquet.

AMELIA [*quietly*]. You did not buy me one.

BECKY. It's true her dress is not very distinguished, George. You must send her to my *corsetière*. I'll give you the address.

GEORGE. Ah, it takes you to know what clothes are, Mrs Crawley. Lord, your partners! Lord Bareacres, General Tufto, and . . .

BECKY [*bowing*]. And you, Captain Osborne.

GEORGE [*getting out cigar*]. I saw the Duke smile at you.

BECKY [*ecstatically*]. The Duke!

AMELIA. I must go to bed. [GEORGE *lights cigar*.

RAWDON. Oh, ridiculous, Mrs Osborne. Why, George and I have——

BECKY. No, Rawdon. No gambling in my drawing-room, if you please, you naughty men.

RAWDON. I owe Osborne his revenge.

GEORGE. By Gad, he does, and everything succeeds with me to-night, too. I've been to the Duchess' ball. I've danced with Becky, I've——

BECKY [*exaggeratedly*]. I forbid cards in my rooms, Captain Osborne. And you are smoking, sir.

GEORGE. Upon my word, I forgot. I forget everything to-night [*going to throw cigar away*].

BECKY. Don't throw it away. Downstairs you can smoke with Rawdon.

RAWDON. Yes. I'd like a weed. Come along, Osborne.
[GEORGE *starts towards door*.

AMELIA. George!
[*He looks at her, hesitating.* BECKY *takes the cigar out of his hand; he turns in wonderment to her.*

BECKY. To show that I forgive you. [*She takes a puff and returns it to him.*]

GEORGE. Jove! Finest cigar I ever smoked in the world. [*He ignores* AMELIA.]

[RAWDON *puts hand on* GEORGE's *shoulder and takes him up C. Exeunt* RAWDON *and* GEORGE.

BECKY. Amelia, oh, you poor dear, how tired you look!

AMELIA [*indignantly*]. Tired!

BECKY. Yes, dear, I know you are not used to late hours, but I could not let you go to bed without warning you.

AMELIA. Warning me? You!

BECKY. Oh, my dearest, do sit down. [*Both sit on settee.*] You must listen to your Rebecca. You must. For God's sake, child, stop your husband's gambling or he will ruin himself. He and Rawdon are at cards every night. Why don't you prevent it, you little careless creature? Why don't you come to us of an evening where you could exercise some control?

AMELIA. Could I?

BECKY. Well, I hope so.

AMELIA. Would you let me?

BECKY. *I* let you!

AMELIA. Rebecca, did I ever do you anything but kindness?

BECKY. Indeed, no. That is why I am so anxious to do you a kindness now.

AMELIA. By coming between my husband and me? By separating those whom God hath joined and taking my darling's heart from me?

BECKY [*rising*]. Oh, heavens! This is injustice. George has a weakness for play. I dare to mention it and you insinuate the most cruel things. Oh, Amelia!

AMELIA [*rising*]. What have I done to you that you should try to take him from me?

BECKY. I? Do *I* want him? What qualities has he that I should find attractive? True, he has heavenly feet. He danced divinely to-night, did he not?

AMELIA. How should I know? He did not dance with me, his wife.

BECKY. Dearest, isn't that just what I warn you of?

AMELIA. Do you think I couldn't see it for myself?

BECKY. My dear, you can't. You don't. He danced with me. But why? Not for my sake. Not because he admires me. I overheard him tell one of the dandies that I was the most distinguished woman at the ball, and when his friend said I was a neat little filly George protested such language was inappropriate to a lady who was related to the Montmorencys. But George did not mean a word of it, my dear. It isn't I who attract him. It's my husband and those wicked, wicked cards. That is why George is amiable—not to me, not to your Rebecca. Oh, no! He is amiable to the wife of Captain Crawley because he wants to go on playing cards with Captain Crawley, and you do nothing to prevent it. Listen, Amelia. It isn't enough to have married a man. We women have to hold our husbands by what poor arts we can. Take your dress to-night. Would George have danced with me if your dress had compelled attention? But, my child, it's dowdy. It's positively dowdy. And the reason? George is too busy losing his guineas to my husband to have any to spare for your dressmakers. Don't you see how it all belongs together, how it is all, all George's passion for cards?

AMELIA. You deliberately sent them to play cards now.

BECKY. Oh, the injury you do me! I sent them, I who forbade card-playing in my rooms! My dear, my husband's weak. God forbid that I should speak an ill word of my Rawdon, but he is weak. He is always to be tempted. George tempts him and you will not prevent it. Amelia, do, do make an effort to prevent it. You have only been married six weeks to George: surely your hold on him is strong. And when we are at war, when our husbands are both about to march away and . . . and may not come back.

BECKY SHARP

AMELIA. Oh, Becky! [*Cries in her arms.*]

BECKY. There! There! They will return. Your . . . your brother is still in Brussels? Dear Mr Joseph!

AMELIA. In this hotel.

BECKY. So near? Ah, what a comfort he will be to us when our husbands are away. We weak women need a protector.

AMELIA [*releasing herself from* BECKY'S *arms*]. I think you have offended Joseph.

BECKY. I! Impossible! I have the greatest regard for him.

AMELIA. When he is in the same hotel and you did not know it.

BECKY. My society has been so military.

AMELIA. Oh, your grand friends! Too high for——
[*Bugle sounds off.*

AMELIA. Becky! That means——

BECKY. Yes. [BECKY *stands erect,* AMELIA *clings to her.*] Yes.
[*Door C. opens violently. Enter* JOSEPH SEDLEY, *in dressing-gown.*

JOSEPH. Amelia! I've searched everywhere and I find you here! [*Stiffly*] Your servant, Mrs Crawley.

BECKY [*curtseying*]. Dear Mr Joseph.

JOSEPH. You heard the bugles?

AMELIA. Yes.

JOSEPH. I'd word ten minutes since. They march at three.

AMELIA. At three. Oh, heavens! And it is half-past two.

JOSEPH. Yes. Where's George? It's time he——

BECKY. With Captain Crawley. They will have heard.

JOSEPH. Oh, I envy them. I'd give the world to be a soldier now. I've half a mind——

AMELIA. Joseph! When George must go, would you leave me too?

JOSEPH. I have seen a bit of service in India, you know. I've smelt powder, and——

AMELIA. Oh, don't desert me, Joseph!

JOSEPH. Pooh, my dear creature, there's no danger. The Allies will finish Bonaparte and be in Paris in two months. I'll dine you at the Palais Royal, by Jove. You don't know military affairs, my dear. We've got the Duke, haven't we?

AMELIA. I think of George.

JOSEPH. Damme, George is English. Do you think he's frightened of any man, let alone a Frenchman? Do you think he'll thank you for pulling a long face when he's riding out to victory?

[*Gramophone, off R., plays " The Girl I Left Behind Me."* JOSEPH *goes to window, throws back curtain.*

Why, there's a regiment marching now. [*Prances in step by window.*] Yes, that's the stride. Make mincemeat of them, boys, make mince—— Damme, the Duke. Amelia, it's the Duke himself. [*Salutes.*]

[BECKY *goes to window and waves.*

Oh, it's hard on a man. It's hard to be left behind. [*Comes C.*]

BECKY [*from window*]. Oh, you men! You would sacrifice anything for a pleasure.

JOSEPH. My dear madam, I only said I should like to go. I didn't say I was going.

BECKY [*coming to him*]. You have noble inspirations, Mr Sedley. But the protectorship of weak women, is not that also noble?

JOSEPH. Gad, you're right. I mustn't let my inclinations get the better of me. I have my sister to care for.

BECKY. Yes, and if . . . if we have to fly, there would be a little corner for me in your coach?

JOSEPH. Eh? Fly?

AMELIA. Oh!

JOSEPH [*with elaborate dignity*]. Yes, madam, in the case of so outrageous an improbability you shall have a corner in my coach. [BECKY *breathes a happy sigh*. But to dream of such a thing is monstrous. Monstrous, madam, do you hear? It's un-English. It's——

Enter C. RAWDON *and* GEORGE, *both grave*

RAWDON. What is, Sedley?

JOSEPH [*eyeing* BECKY *indignantly*]. Something, sir, that I will not even mention before you gentlemen.

AMELIA [*to* GEORGE]. George!

GEORGE [*arm round her*]. Amelia! Come. I must change. I must write to my father and you——

AMELIA. I will pray, George.

RAWDON [*curtly*]. Cut him some sandwiches while you pray, Mrs Osborne, and put some brandy in his flask and make him some coffee to drink before we start.

AMELIA. But I——

BECKY. That's good advice.

GEORGE [*taking her out*]. Emmy.

   [*Exeunt* GEORGE *and* AMELIA. JOSEPH *is following, but he hesitates.*

JOSEPH [*turning*]. Damn it, Crawley, you and I have differed. But there, man, there. [*Offers hand.*] Come through it sound.

RAWDON [*shaking*]. I'll try.   [*Exit* JOSEPH. Fat elephant!

BECKY. Isn't he? Had you time to do anything with Osborne?

RAWDON. Two hundred.

BECKY. Good.

RAWDON. He played frantically and I let him. I was thinking of you.

BECKY. Of me?

RAWDON [*giving notes*]. You'd better take it now.

BECKY. But, Rawdon——

RAWDON. My dear, we're marching. I'm a pretty good mark for a shot.

BECKY. Oh!

RAWDON. Well, if I drop——

BECKY. You shan't.

RAWDON. Look here, I'd like to know this before I do. You've made life different for me. I've never been so happy as in the months of our marriage. What did I do before? Turf, ring, hunting, gambling, and—I might as well say it now—women. Then I married you, and damme, Bec, lawful matrimony with you is the finest sport on earth. It's a bad thought for me that if I fall to-day I don't leave you provided for.

BECKY. You won't fall, Rawdon.

RAWDON. Well, let's see what there is for you. [*Sits at head of table.*] You've got Osborne's two hundred. Here's my pocket-book. Another . . . yes—thirty. Take all that, Becky. If I'm hit you know I cost you nothing. [BECKY *cries.*] Don't cry, little woman. I may live to vex you. Now, the horses. I leave you two horses in the stables here. There's the key. Good cattle, too. Say a hundred each. There's my dressing-case in there, cost me two hundred— that is, I owe two hundred for it. Pins, rings, watches. Put 'em all up the spout, my dear. It's a poor lot, but——

BECKY. You're coming back.

RAWDON. I'm going into battle and it's no use blinking facts. [*Rises.*] I'll change these clothes for the shabbiest uniform I've got. You can sell these and—— [*Looks at watch.*] Jove, I must hurry.

BECKY. I must cut sandwiches and get brandy.

RAWDON. I've brandy in there.

BECKY SHARP

BECKY. Then sandwiches. [*He shakes head.*] You told Amelia——

RAWDON. I gave the fool an occupation. You're sounder mettle. Will you prove that?

BECKY. Rawdon, I'll do anything.

RAWDON. It's a big thing. Becky, if I'm going to my death, I'd like to go with the sound of your singing in my ears. I'll leave the bedroom door open while I change. Then I can hear and see you. Becky, will you? Can you?

BECKY [*controlling herself*]. Yes.   [RAWDON *kisses her.*

RAWDON. Gad, you have pluck.

[*Exit L., leaving door open.*
[BECKY *acts strain; as she plays notes at piano, she nearly collapses on keyboard; then recovers and sings a song through.*

RAWDON [*returning in shabby uniform*]. I haven't a moment. Becky, you're wonderful.

[*Embraces her quickly and exit C.*

BECKY. Rawdon! [*Looks at door, then at her dress.*] And I . . . I'm in a ball dress.

[*She begins to undo it and goes off L.*
[*Drums and bugle off.*

CURTAIN

SCENE II: *Curtain rises on the same scene. Early evening of June* 18. *Window-curtains drawn. Table laid for three.*

Enter C. JOSEPH *and* AMELIA, JOSEPH *in a heavily braided, half-military coat, carrying hat.*

AMELIA [*comes in reluctantly*]. Becky's not here, Joseph. I'm sure I don't want——   [*Turning to door as if to go.*]

JOSEPH. Rubbish, Amelia. You'll stay where you're invited and where you accepted.

AMELIA. *You* accepted.

JOSEPH. Did I? Well, I'm in charge of you. Damme, girl, do you think I *want* to dine with Becky Sharp?

AMELIA. Then——

JOSEPH. But I want to *dine*. I haven't had a square meal since the troops marched away.

AMELIA. Oh! [*Handkerchief out.*]

JOSEPH. Oh, Lord, she's off again. There! There! Stupid of me to have reminded you. But why can't you bear up better—like Becky?

AMELIA. I will try, Joseph.

JOSEPH. Do. I've enough to worry me in a hotel full of caterwauling natives running about like frightened sheep. I'll undertake to say it would take more than a war to upset a good English Inn as this place is upset. I can't get service. [*Looks at table.*] But Becky can.

AMELIA. She speaks French so well.

JOSEPH. French! Damme, I swear at them in Hindutanee and I can't get attention.

AMELIA. No, Joseph. But then in Brussels they are not Hindus: they're Belgians.

JOSEPH. Lost all control of themselves because Boney's near. [*Snaps fingers impatiently.*] Where is Becky? I'm hungry.

Enter BECKY *L.*

BECKY [*swimming to* AMELIA *and kissing her*]. Dearest Amelia. . . . Oh, Mr Sedley, your coat!

JOSEPH. My coat, madam! It's a very fine coat.

BECKY. But braided. It's like your moustache. So terrifyingly martial.

JOSEPH. It needn't terrify you.

BECKY. But it does. It tells me you are going to join the army and leave us to our fate.

JOSEPH. No, no.

BECKY. Ah, but I know it. You are bent on plunging into the frenzied scene.

JOSEPH [*pulling moustache, flattered*]. Haw—every man of spirit would. But my duty keeps me here.

AMELIA. I am so greatly relieved. I thought you were deserting us just when our need of you is urgent.

JOSEPH. Urgent?

AMELIA. That bell.

JOSEPH. Well?

BECKY. I ring but no one answers. [*Rings.*] Oh, I will try again, but no one will come.

JOSEPH. You mean the servants . . . but that table, that laid table?

BECKY. A whited sepulchre. They laid it, then ran into the streets for news. Is it not dreadful when I have guests?

JOSEPH. There is no dinner?

BECKY. None.

JOSEPH. Good heaven!

BECKY. Shops . . . shops are open, Mr Joseph. But what can a woman do? I can't go out into those maddened streets of Brussels, and . . . and we women, we wives, we cry but we can't eat tears. [*Goes to window.*] See, just below, there is a shop open.

JOSEPH. I will see what I can do. [*Gets hat.*]

BECKY. Oh, what a thing it is to be a *man*. If it were only bread and cheese. [*At door C.*]

JOSEPH. Bread and cheese!

BECKY. And . . . and anything else you can procure. I have wine. [*Exit* JOSEPH. BECKY *closes door.*

AMELIA [*accusingly*]. Becky, you——

BECKY. Do not be agitated, dear Amelia. Joseph will feed the hungry.

AMELIA. Yes. That is why you invited us. You knew the servants had deserted.

BECKY. When gentlemen take pleasure in obliging us, my sweet, it is our womanly duty to provide them with opportunities of serving us.

AMELIA. Your womanly duty! Oh, you confess it! You are using him.

BECKY. Would you have us false to our husbands, Amelia?

AMELIA. What!

BECKY. Did they not go away happy in the knowledge that we were protected by the lion-hearted Mr Joseph? Oh, Amelia, you who have father, mother, brother, all! What can you know, how should you judge of the necessities of a poor friendless orphan? To grudge me the little kindnesses of Mr Joseph! It was ungenerous of you.

AMELIA. You always put me in the wrong.

BECKY. My dearest friend thoughtlessly put herself in the wrong. Own that you were ungenerous, my darling.

AMELIA [*hesitates, then—*] Yes.

BECKY [*with a sly smile*]. Ah. [*She goes to table, takes up wine and corkscrew.*] [*Sound of cannon off.*

AMELIA. What's that?

BECKY. *C'est le feu.*

AMELIA. Heaven defend us, it's cannon. [*She runs to window.*]

BECKY [*coolly uncorking bottle, pours*]. Nearer. Much nearer than they were.

> [JOSEPH *enters C., in panic. He carries a long loaf and cheese and puts them on table. During the ensuing,* BECKY *calmly eats and drinks.*

[*Sitting*] Oh, thank you, Mr Joseph.

JOSEPH. Thank me? Good Gad, madam, the news in the *pâtisserie*!

BECKY SHARP

AMELIA [*coming from window*]. News! Joseph, what is it?

JOSEPH. Help me off with this coat quick.

AMELIA. Your coat!

JOSEPH. Frogged. Braided in the military fashion.

BECKY. So that people who did not look very closely might take you for a soldier, Mr Joseph, with your military figure and your fierce moustache and——

JOSEPH. The French have sworn not to give quarter to a single British soldier.

BECKY. I have it! Turn the coat inside out.

JOSEPH. Lord, what a brain you have. Saved! Saved! [*turning sleeves, then putting it on*].

AMELIA. Saved from what? What is the news?

JOSEPH. There was a Belgian hussar in the *pâtisserie*, fled from the field. The only man of his regiment, the rest all slain. He's told me the most terrible news. We must fly for our lives.

AMELIA. Fly!

JOSEPH. The town's in panic. They say the Duke's a prisoner. The Belgians ran and——

AMELIA. And George? Had the man seen George?

JOSEPH. No. But all's over, Emmy. The French will be here in an hour. I won't stop to be butchered by a Frenchman. Come. [*Takes her wrist.*]

AMELIA. Without my husband, Joseph?

JOSEPH. Damn it, don't you understand? The Allies are defeated. We must fly to Ghent and——

AMELIA. I shall await my husband. Alive or dead, he will come to me here. [*Frees herself.*]

JOSEPH. But Bonaparte is——

AMELIA. I am going to my room.

[*Exit* AMELIA *C., she closes door in his face.*

JOSEPH. Good-bye, then, and be——

BECKY [*who has risen and stands between him and door*]. Mr Joseph.

JOSEPH. Oh, I've no time for you. [*Pushing her.*]

BECKY. No. But will you fly on wings?

JOSEPH. I've got my coach.

BECKY. And horses? And horses, Mr Joseph?

JOSEPH [*backing from her*]. Good God! All the horses are with the army.

BECKY. You'll have to walk. But then, you'll be quite safe now you've turned your coat.

JOSEPH. Walk! A man of my habit walk! I'd pay a hundred pound for a horse.

BECKY. The people who have horses in Brussels to-night are few. Few and so very, very fortunate. Is not that always the case when an article is scarce and there are many eager purchasers?

JOSEPH. Are there horses at all? Becky, if you know of any, where? Where?

BECKY. Captain Crawley happened to leave two behind.

JOSEPH. Rawdon! Oh, what foresight! We are saved, saved. Where are they?

BECKY. Locked in the stable of this hotel.

JOSEPH. And the key? Quick! Where's the key?

BECKY. The key is where I have put it, Mr Sedley.

JOSEPH. Give it me. I'll have them out at once and——

BECKY. *Give*, Mr Sedley? Give? Do you know I've just refused to sell to Lady Bareacres at twelve hundred?

JOSEPH. You wanted them, yourself.

BECKY [*shaking head*]. I'm not going.

JOSEPH. Not going? But the French are at the gates of Brussels.

BECKY. If they are, Mr Sedley, I still don't go.

JOSEPH. Oh, you trust to their sparing women. But I shall get no quarter. I'm a man.

BECKY SHARP

BECKY. They will perceive it by—your coat.

JOSEPH. Becky, Mrs Crawley, have you thought what may happen to women when the dastardly and brutal French reach Brussels?

BECKY. Are you trying to frighten me? Mr Sedley, it was once said of Becky Sharp that she couldn't be a born woman of fashion: her French accent was too good.

JOSEPH. Well?

BECKY [*with gesture*]. Well!

JOSEPH. You'd pretend to be French!

BECKY [*piously*]. I should trust to God and to my taste in clothes, which is so unlike our dear Amelia's.

JOSEPH. But the horses . . . for me.

BECKY. I mentioned that Lady Bareacres offered twelve hundred.

JOSEPH. Twelve hundred pound for a pair of horses! [*Cunningly*] Oh, but she'd to drive. I'll ride. One is enough for me.

BECKY. Both or neither, Mr Sedley.

JOSEPH. Good God! Twelve hundred pound!

BECKY. That was what I had to refuse, even from a countess, in accordance with the commands of my dear husband. He ordered me not to part with them for less than fifteen hundred.

> [JOSEPH *makes a gesture; he sits heavily on settee.*
> BECKY *runs to window.*

Lud, what's that in the street?

JOSEPH [*not moving*]. What is it?

BECKY. How the people run. All in one direction. All away from Bonaparte.

JOSEPH [*groaning*]. Fifteen hundred pound.

BECKY [*speaking from window*]. It is no doubt in your pocket. We all carry our wealth on our persons here, do we not?

JOSEPH. Becky, if you had any regard for me——

BECKY. I think the streets grow worse. Heavens, is that a French uniform I see!

JOSEPH [*starting to window*]. French!

BECKY [*shuddering back from window*]. Oh, God! I can look no more.

JOSEPH [*as they meet, C.*]. The horses! The horses! Give me the stable key.

BECKY. I sell it. For fifteen hundred.

JOSEPH. Becky, I'll pay a thousand. You're . . . you're teasing and there isn't time.

BECKY. I'm a monopolist of horses, Mr Sedley, and I may be a widow at this moment. I must think of my future. Of course, if the French catch you, your future——

JOSEPH [*takes out pocket-book*]. Oh, Becky, there—there's a thousand. I implore you, on my knee . . . the key . . . [*Kneels.*] Dear sweet creature, take the thousand and give me the key. [*He kneels facing audience.*]

[*Door opens.* RAWDON, *his clothes dusty, is coming in. Over* JOSEPH's *head* BECKY *makes violent gestures to him to go. He goes, closing door.*

JOSEPH. Who was that?

BECKY. That, my dear Mr Sedley, was some one else who knows I've got those horses. Shall I call him in?

JOSEPH. Don't do that. For God's sake don't do that. There! See, I'm getting out the other five hundred.

BECKY [*as he is still kneeling, taking his scarf-pin*]. I'll have this too.

JOSEPH [*scrambling up*]. But that's a diamond. It's worth——

BECKY. Pooh! A souvenir of our bargain, or . . . shall I call the other gentleman?

JOSEPH. No, no. Here are the notes. [*Gives.*]

BECKY SHARP

BECKY [*takes key from her bosom*]. And here is the key.

JOSEPH. Ah! [*Snatches it and goes to door, opens, then turns.*] Vixen!

BECKY [*laughing, laying out notes on table one by one with a staccato gesture for each*]. All's fair in war.

JOSEPH. Is it? [*Suddenly angry.*] Then what is to prevent my retaking my money? I'm stronger than you. [*Coming down.*]

BECKY. Are you? [*Dodging him, up to door, she opens and calls*] Rawdon! [*Enter* RAWDON.

JOSEPH [*backing*]. Captain Crawley!

RAWDON. No, sir. Colonel Crawley, promoted on the field of victory.

JOSEPH. Victory! But I heard—I spoke with a man——

RAWDON. I have ridden with despatches from the Duke, sir. The French are on the run from Waterloo.

BECKY. Rawdon, you're unhurt. [*Her arms round his neck.*]

RAWDON. Except by Mr Sedley. Mr Sedley, whom I find, while we soldiers are away, forcing his foul attentions on my wife and——

JOSEPH. No, no. I'll explain. It wasn't that at all, it——

RAWDON. Go, sir. Go before I whip you.

JOSEPH. But—— [RAWDON *points to door. Exit* JOSEPH.

BECKY. You heard?

RAWDON [*smiling*]. Quite enough.

BECKY. We . . . we poor people have to live. Look. [*Shows the notes spread on table.*]

RAWDON. What! Fifteen hundred!

BECKY. The price of your horses. For Mr Sedley to escape the French!

RAWDON. Gad, Becky, you're wonderful. What a time we'll have in Paris.

BECKY. Out there was your victory, my colonel. This is mine.

> [*He embraces her.* JOSEPH *opens door and speaks without coming in.*

JOSEPH. Mrs Crawley, I do not consider you a nice woman.

BECKY [*releases herself from* RAWDON, *then curtseys elaborately*]. No, Mr Sedley, I am Becky Sharp.

CURTAIN

Applications regarding amateur performances of this play should be addressed to Messrs Samuel French, Ltd., 26 Southampton Street, Strand, London, W.C.2, or to Mr Le Roy Phillips, 41 Winter Street, Boston, Massachusetts, U.S.A.

$X = 0$
A NIGHT OF THE TROJAN WAR
A POETIC PLAY
By John Drinkwater

Mr John Drinkwater is a famous poet as well as a fine dramatist, and it is fitting that "$X = 0$: A Night of the Trojan War" is written in blank verse. He is still young, but has already achieved great success. Everybody knows his "Abraham Lincoln," "Oliver Cromwell," and "Robert E. Lee." The chief thing to be said about Mr Drinkwater is that he has rediscovered the uses of the chronicle play, although his "Mary Stuart" cannot be included in this category. His plays have been extremely successful on both sides of the Atlantic. He has also done excellent work as one of the co-founders of the Birmingham Repertory Theatre.

CHARACTERS

PRONAX } Greeks
SALVIUS

ILUS } Trojans
CAPYS

A GREEK SENTINEL
A GREEK SERVANT

The action passes between a Greek tent and the Trojan walls, and is continuous.

This play was first produced at the Birmingham Repertory Theatre on Saturday, April 14, 1917, under the direction of the author, with the following cast:

Pronax . . . . FELIX AYLMER
Salvius . . . . NICHOLAS BLY
Ilus . . . . . JOSEPH A. DODD
Capys . . . . WILLIAM J. REA
A Greek Sentinel . ALFRED J. BROOKS
A Greek Servant . RICHARD WAYNE

The setting was devised by Frank D. Clewlow.

$X = 0$

A NIGHT OF THE TROJAN WAR

Scene I: *A Grecian tent on the plain before Troy, towards the end of the ten years' war. It is a starry summer night.* PRONAX *and* SALVIUS, *two young Greek soldiers, are in the tent,* SALVIUS *reading by a lighted torch,* PRONAX *watching the night. During the scene a* SENTINEL *passes at intervals to and fro behind the tent.*

PRONAX. So is the night often at home. I have seen
White orchards brighten under a summer moon,
As now these tents under the stars. This hour
My father's coppices are full of song,
While sleep is on the comfortable house—
Unless one dear one wakes to think of me
And count my chances when the Trojan death
Goes on its nightly errand.
                     [*The* SENTINEL *passes.*
             It's a dear home,
And fragrant, and there's blessed fruit and corn,
And thoughts that make me older than my youth
Come even from the nettles at the gate.
To-day, perhaps, the harvesters are out,
And on the night is the ripe pollen blown. . . .
And this is the third harvest that has gone
While we have wasted on a barren plain
To avenge some wrong done in our babyhood
On beauty that we have not seen. Three years . . .

But so it is, and so it must be done,
Till the Greek oath is proven. Salvius,
Why is all lovely thought a pain?
    SALVIUS.   We know
Even upon the flood of adoration,
That beauty passes. That's the tragic tale
That is our world.
    PRONAX.   Is it not very strange
That, prisoned in this quarrel so long and long,
Until to remember a little Argive street
Is torture to the bone, yet there is now
Nothing of hatred in the blood for them
Whose death is all our daily use, but merely
Consent in death, knowing that death may strike
Across our tongues as lightly as those that lie
For ever dumb because we might not spare?
    SALVIUS. Not strange; who goes in company with death,
Watching his daily desolation, thinking,
On every stroke, of all the agony
That from that stroke goes throbbing, throbbing, throbbing,
Forgets all hate. How should we hate the dead?
And, where death ranges as among us now,
You, Pronax, I, and our antagonists
And friends alike are all but as dead men
                                        [*The* SENTINEL *passes.*
Moving together in a ghostly world,
With life a luckless beggar at the door.
It is not ours to hate, who have all put by
That safety where men think eternity
Immeasurably far, and leisured passions have
Their sorry breeding place. Great kings may hate,
And priests may thunder hate, and grey-beard prophets
May cry again to those who cry their hate
In pride of their new-found authority,

$X = 0$

Fearing lest love should mark them as they are,
And send them barren from their brutal thrift.
But not for us this envy.   It is ours
Merely to die, or give the death that these
Out of their hatred or indifference will.

PRONAX. It's not that a man grows tardy in his duty. . . .
It's still a glad thing to do as the motherland bids,
Though the blind soul forgets how sprang the cause.
I shall die in my hour, though it should come to-day,
Not grudging.   Yet it is bitterness for youth,
When nothing should be but scrutiny of life,
Mating, and building towards a durable fame,
And setting the hearthstone trim for a lover's cares,
To let all knowledge of these things go, and learn
Only of death, that should be hidden from youth,
A great thing biding upon the fulness of age,
And not made common gossip among these tides
Of daily beastliness.   And still I must remember,
For all I have renounced my thronging life,
My orchards, and my rivers, and the bells
Of twilight cattle moving in the mist.

SALVIUS. I know; the mind grows faint with thinking
  of them—
Those little, lovely things of home.   My bed
Looks to the west on the Ionian sea—
A sweet, fresh-smelling room it is.   I wrote
My rightest poems there.   I cannot see
A sail now coming Troyward but my brain
Is sick for that small room, above the quay
Where sailors laugh at dawn and all day long,
Until the silent sunset ships go out
Into Sicilian waters.

PRONAX.   There your poems
Were made, in Pylos; and in Athens I

Too dreamed, although I caught no lyric song—
I envy you your song;—I was to build
A cleaner state; I dreamed a policy
Purer than states have known; I was to bring
Princedom to every hearth, to every man
Knowledge that he was master of his fate.
The dream is dulled. Three years of Trojan dust
Have taught me but to pray at night for sleep,
And an arm stronger in cunning than my foe's,
A quicker eye to parry death. And, Salvius,
What of your songs?
    SALVIUS.   Asleep these many days,
Biding their happy time if that should be.
    PRONAX. And death is watching,   [*The* SENTINEL *passes*.
                              and your song, that grew
In the womb of generations for the use
And joy of men, may perish ere it takes
Its larger music, that the tale may go
That Greece drove bloodier war than Ilium;
That's a poor bargain. . . . But these thoughts that stir
Like ghosts out of a life that should have been,
Neglect my duty. It is past the hour
I should be nosing along the Trojan wall
To catch what prey may be. I have scarred the wall
At the bend there where I told you, in the breaking stone,
These many nights, until at last I've made
A foothold to the top. It's a queer game,
This tripping of life suddenly in the dark,
This blasting of flesh that is wholesome yet in the blood,
And those who weep, I think, are as those would weep
If I should fall. I loathe it; but, good-night;
You should sleep; it is late, and it is your guard at dawn.
      [*He is arming himself, and wrapping himself in his
         cloak.*

$X = 0$

Good-night. What are you reading?
  SALVIUS.   Songs that one
Made in my province. The sails are in his song,
And seabirds, and our level pasture-lands,
And the bronzed fishers on the flowing tides.
His name was Creon. I will make such songs
If the years will.
  PRONAX [*who has poured himself out and drunk a cup of wine*].   I know. Put out the torch
If you're abed before I come. Good-night.
  SALVIUS. Good-night : good luck.
  PRONAX.   And will you bid them fill
The trough; this business may make bloody hands.
                 [*He looks out into the night, and goes.*
                          [*The* SENTINEL *passes.*
  SALVIUS [*reading*]. Upon the dark Sicilian waves,
              The casting fishers go. . . .

CURTAIN

SCENE II: *On Troy wall.* CAPYS, *a young Trojan soldier, is on guard, looking out over the plain where the Greeks are encamped.* ILUS, *another young soldier, his friend, wearing a bearskin, comes to him.*

  ILUS. When does your watch end?
  CAPYS.   In two hours; at midnight.
  ILUS. They're beautiful, those tents, under the stars.
It is my night to go like a shadow among them,
And, snatching a Greek life, come like a shadow again.
It's an odd skill to have won in the rose of your youth—

Two years, and once in seven days—a hundred,
More than a hundred, and only once a fault.
A hundred Greek boys, Capys, like myself—
Loving, and quick in honour, and clean of fear—
Spoiled in their beauty by me whose desire is beauty
Since first I walked the April hedgerows. Would time
But work upon this Helen's face, maybe
This nine-year quarrel would be done, and Troy
Grow sane, and her confounding councillors
Be given carts to clean and drive to market.
What of your sea-girl? Has she grown?

CAPYS. You ask
Always the question, friend. The chisels rust,
The moths are in my linen coats, my mallets
Are broken. Ilus, in my brain were limbs
Supple and mighty; the beauty of women moved
To miraculous birth in my imagining;
I had conceived the body of man, to make
Divine articulation of the joy
That flows uncounted in every happy step
Of health; the folk faring about Troy streets
Should have flowered upon my marble marvellously
I would have given my land a revelation
Sweet as the making of it had been to me.
And still it shall be, if ever from my mind
Falls this obscure monotony, that makes
The world an echo, its vivid gesture gone.
Troy peaceful shall be Troy magnificent,
For I will make her so.

ILUS. It would be grand
If Troy would use us as we might be used,
To build and sing and make her market-places
Honest, and show her people that all evil
Is the lethargic mind. I have seen this Troy

$X = 0$

Bloom in my thought into a simple state
Where jealousy was dead because no man spoke
Out of his vanity of the thing he knew not.
Capys, it is so little that is needed
For righteousness ; we are all so truly made,
If only to our making we were true.
Why should we fight these Greeks ?   There was some
    anger,
Some generous heat of the blood those years ago
When Paris brought his Helen into Troy
With Menelaus screaming at his heels ;
But that's forgotten now, and none can stay
This thing that none would have endure.   I have thought
Often, upon those nights when I have gone
Fatally through the Grecian tents, how well
Might he whose life I stole and I have thriven
Together conspiring this or that of good
For all men, and I have sickened, and gone on
To strike again as Troy has bidden me,
For an oath is a queer weevil in the brain.
  CAPYS. Who's there ?
  A VOICE.   Troy and the Trojan death.
  CAPYS.   Pass Troy.
It is still upon the plains to-night, and the stars
Are a lantern light against you—you must go
Warily, Ilus.   The loss of many friends
Has sharpened my love, not dulled me against loss.
I am careful for you to-night in all this beauty
Of glowing summer—disaster might choose this night
So brutally, and so disaster likes.
Go warily.
  ILUS.   I know the tented squares
And every lane among the Greeks, as I know
The walls of Troy ; and I can pass at night

Within an handshot of a watching eye,
And be but a shadow of cloud or a windy bush.
A hundred times, remember.
    CAPYS.   Yet would I could come
To take your danger or share it.
    ILUS.   No ; there's a use
That's more than courage in this. And, Capys, yet
Those chisels must win your vision into form
For the world's light and ease. It's an ill day
Among ill days that smites the seer's lips.
Your work's to do.
    CAPYS.   And yours—that dream of Troy
Regenerate, with the heart of the people shown
In the people's life, not lamentably hurt
By men who, mazed with authority, put by
Authority's proper use, and so are evil,
While still the folk under their tyranny keep
Their kindness, waiting upon deliverance.
So may we come together to our work,
In prophecy you of life, creation I.
How long to-night ?
    ILUS.   Before your watch is done
I shall be back. Here at this point, before
The night is full ; throw me the rope upon
The signal, thus——
        [*He whistles. He is climbing over the parapet, to
           which he has hooked a rope.*
                    Peace with you till I come.
  CAPYS. And luck with you. Go warily. Farewell.
      [ILUS *drops down to the plain below.* CAPYS *draws the
        rope up. There is silence for a moment.*
  CAPYS [*moving to and fro along the wall*].
      Or Greek or Trojan, all is one
        When snow falls on our summertime,

And when the happy noonday rhyme
Because of death is left undone.

The bud that breaks must surely pass,
Yet is the bud more sure of May
Than youth of age, when every day
Death is youth's shadow in the glass.

> [*A hand is seen groping on the parapet.*
> PRONAX, *looking cautiously along the wall,
> draws himself up silently, unseen by* CAPYS,
> *who continues.*

Beside us ever moves a hand,
Unseen, of deadly stroke, and when
It falls on youth——

> [*He hears the movement behind him, and
> turns swiftly.*

Who's there?

PRONAX [*rushing upon him*]. A Greek unlucky to Trojan arms—

A sworn Greek, terrible in obedience.

> [*His onslaught has overwhelmed* CAPYS, *who falls
> without a cry, the Greek's dagger in his breast.*
> PRONAX *draws it out, looks at his dead antagonist,
> shudders, peers out over the wall, and very care-
> fully climbs down at the point where he came.*

CURTAIN

SCENE III: *The Greek tent again.* SALVIUS *is still reading,
and the torch burning. A* SERVANT *brings a large jar of
water which he pours into the trough outside the tent. He
goes with the jar, and a moment later the* SENTINEL *passes*

behind the tent. There is silence for a few moments, SALVIUS *turning the pages of his book. Then, from the shadow in front of the tent,* ILUS *in his bearskin is seen stealthily approaching. He reaches the tent opening without a sound, and in the same unbroken silence his dagger is in the Greek's heart.* ILUS *catches the dead man as he falls, and lets his body sink on to one of the couches inside the tent. The* SENTINEL *passes.* ILUS, *breathless, waits till the steps have gone, and then, stealthily as he came, disappears.*

There is a pause. PRONAX *comes out of the darkness, and, throwing his cloak on the ground, goes straight to the trough, and begins to wash his hands.*

PRONAX. What, still awake, and reading? Those are rare songs,
To keep a soldier out of his bed at night.
Ugh—Salvius, sometimes it's horrible—
He had no time for a word—he walked those walls
Under the stars as a lover might walk a garden
Among the moonlit roses—this cleansing's good—
He was saying some verses, I think, till death broke in.
Cold water's good after this pitiful doing,
And freshens the mind for comfortable sleep.
Well, there, it's done, and sleep's a mighty curer
For all vexations. [*The* SENTINEL *passes.*
        It's time that torch was out—
I do not need it, and you should be abed. . . .
Salvius . . .
      [*He looks into the tent for the first time.*
      What, sleeping, and still dressed?
That's careless, friend, and the torch alight still. . . .
      Salvius . . .
Salvius, I say . . . gods! . . . what, friend . . .

$X = 0$

Salvius, Salvius . . .
Dead . . . it is done . . . it is done . . . there is judgment made. . . .
Beauty is broken . . . and there on the Trojan wall
One too shall come . . . one too shall come . . .

[*The* SENTINEL *passes.*

CURTAIN

SCENE IV : *The Trojan wall. The body of* CAPYS *lies in the starlight and silence. After a few moments the signal comes from* ILUS *below. There is a pause. The signal is repeated. There is a pause.*

CURTAIN

Applications regarding performances of this play should be made to the author, Mr John Drinkwater, c/o Messrs Sidgwick and Jackson, Ltd., 3 Adam Street, Adelphi, London, W.C.2